ROUTLEDGE LIBRARY EDITIONS:
ACCOUNTING

Volume 61

ACCOUNTING IN SCOTLAND

ACCOUNTING IN SCOTLAND

A Historical Bibliography

Compiled by
JANET E. PRYCE-JONES

Annotated by
R. H. PARKER

Routledge
Taylor & Francis Group
LONDON AND NEW YORK

First published by the Institute of Chartered Accountants of Scotland in 1974
Second edition published 1976

This edition first published in 2014
by Routledge
2 Park Square, Milton Park, Abingdon, Oxon, OX14 4RN

and by Routledge
711 Third Avenue, New York, NY 10017

Routledge is an imprint of the Taylor & Francis Group, an informa business

British Library Cataloguing in Publication Data
A catalogue record for this book is available from the British Library

ISBN: 978-0-415-53081-1 (Set)
eISBN: 978-1-315-88628-2 (Set)
ISBN: 978-0-415-72013-7 (Volume 61)
eISBN: 978-1-315-86713-7 (Volume 61)

Publisher's Note
The publisher has gone to great lengths to ensure the quality of this book but points out that some imperfections in the original copies may be apparent.

Disclaimer
The publisher has made every effort to trace copyright holders and would welcome correspondence from those they have been unable to trace.

ACCOUNTING IN SCOTLAND

A Historical Bibliography

2nd edition

compiled by

Janet E. Pryce-Jones, B.Sc., Grad. I.M.A., A.L.A.

annotated by

R. H. Parker, B.Sc.(Econ.), F.C.A.

The Institute of Chartered Accountants of Scotland

Scottish Committee on Accounting History

27 Queen Street,
Edinburgh,
EH2 1LA

1976

ACKNOWLEDGMENTS

This bibliography, the first project of the Scottish Committee on Accounting History, could not have been compiled without the financial assistance of the following, for which we are very grateful:-

The Institute of Chartered Accountants of Scotland

Arthur Andersen and Co.

Arthur Young McClelland Moores and Co.

Deloitte and Co.

Thomson McLintock and Co.

Mann Judd Gordon and Co.

Meston and Co.

Moody Stuart and Robertson

Peat, Marwick, Mitchell and Co.

Scott, Peden and Co.

University of Dundee.

We should also like to thank all the librarians who have allowed us access to their reserve collections and to other restricted areas, offered much advice and been altogether very helpful. We also thank the Department of Librarianship at the University of Strathclyde for their assistance.

ABOUT THE AUTHORS

Janet E. Pryce-Jones was born in Ilford, Essex, in 1948 and was educated at Wanstead County High School and Queen Mary College, London University, where she read mathematics. Worked in the telecommunications industry for three years before entering Strathclyde University to study for a Post Graduate Diploma in Librarianship. This bibliography is her first project since obtaining her diploma. She later became an Associate of the Library Association and is now mathematics specialist librarian at North East London Polytechnic.

R. H. Parker was born in North Walsham, Norfolk, and educated at University College, London, where he read economics. Qualified as an English chartered accountant in 1958 and has since practised and taught accounting in a number of countries. Author of Management Accounting: an Historical Perspective (1969) and other books. Since 1970 Professor of Accountancy in the University of Dundee. Convener of the Scottish Committee on Accounting History. He takes up an appointment as Professor of Accountancy in the University of Exeter in October, 1976.

SBN 85099 023 8 1st edition, 1974; 2nd edition, 1976.

SCOTTISH COMMITTEE ON ACCOUNTING HISTORY
(1976)

Professor R.H. Parker, B.Sc.(Econ.), F.C.A., University of Dundee (Convener)

* R. Donaldson, M.A., Ph.D., The National Library of Scotland

Anna B.G. Dunlop, M.A., Dip.Ed., A.L.A., The Institute of Chartered Accountants of Scotland

Professor T.A. Lee, M.Sc., C.A., A.T.I.I., University of Edinburgh

≠ N.T. Phillipson, M.A., Ph.D., University of Edinburgh

R.C. Smith, J.P., M.A., C.A.

J.C. Stewart, C.A.

T. Robertson, F.C.A. (Secretary), University of Edinburgh

* 1971 - 1974 J.H. Loudon, M.A.

≠ 1971 - 1975 W. Vamplew, B.Sc.(Soc. Sci.), Ph.D.

FOREWORD

The first Scottish book on accounting was published in 1683. That book heralded a century during which Scotland established its reputation as a land of accountants: a steady stream of textbooks, including some which ran to so many editions that they could be called classics, appeared from Scottish presses.

This bibliography is the first publication of the Scottish Committee on Accounting History, which The Institute of Chartered Accountants of Scotland set up in 1971 "to promote the study of accounting history and to establish and maintain contact with accounting historians and with other committees on accounting history throughout the world".

It is hoped that the bibliography, the first for Scotland in this field, will serve the needs of those interested in Scottish accounting and economic history.

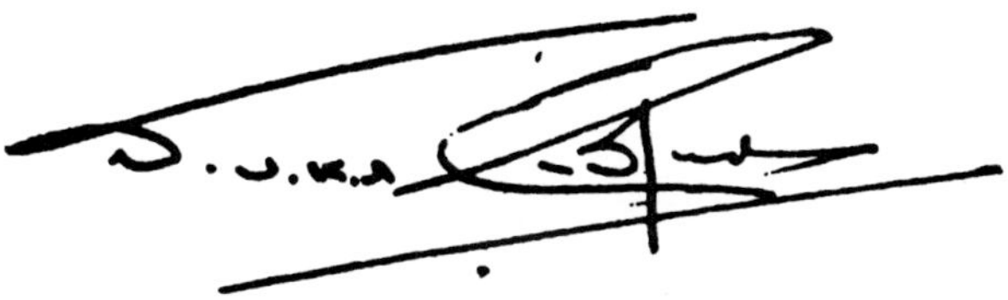

President,
The Institute of Chartered Accountants of Scotland
March 1974

PREFACE TO SECOND EDITION

The first edition (1974), which went out of print early in 1976, received a sufficiently good reception as to encourage us to prepare a second edition. We have been able to include numerous additional items. There are over 330 more location entries (most of them outside the scope of the original project), including 57 libraries other than those originally surveyed. Of the new locations 32 are overseas libraries: these are not claimed to be comprehensive, but we hope they will be useful. There are 35 more main entries and over 50 new entries for further editions.

We are indebted to a number of readers of the first edition and in particular:-

J.C. Stewart, C.A., (a Past President of The Institute of Chartered Accountants of Scotland and a member of the Scottish Committee on Accounting History) who provided us with a number of references which he encountered in the course of his background reading for another of the Committee's projects, a biographical study, which he is preparing, of the 346 "Pioneers of a Profession", the C.A.s of the first 25 years (1854 - 1879) of chartered accountancy in Scotland;

A. Law, O.B.E., M.A., Ph.D., who gave us advice based on his researches into 18th century Scottish school textbooks;

M.J. Mepham, B.Sc. (Econ.), F.C.A. (Heriot-Watt University) who, in addition to notifying us of some new entries, allowed us to make use of his research into the work of John Mair, in a forthcoming article on that author in which Mr Mepham has collaborated with Williard E. Stone, Ph.D., C.P.A.; and

P.J. Wallis, M.A., F.R.Hist.S., F.I.M.A. (Director of Project for Historical Biobibliography, School of Education, University of Newcastle-upon-Tyne), to whom we owe a particular debt of gratitude, since he made available to us a considerable number of locations, extracted from his own research project.

Further changes in the second edition have been necessitated by a transfer of books from Aberdeen and Glasgow to the Institute's Antiquarian Collection in its Edinburgh Library.

CONTENTS

Introduction to Second Edition viii
Abbreviations ix
Part I: Books published in Scotland, 1683 - 1920 1
: Appendix to Part I - Books advertised 51
Part II: Printed Transcriptions of Accounts
(i) Books 53
(ii) Periodical articles 61
Part III: History of Scottish Accounting
(i) Books 64
(ii) Periodical articles 67
(iii) Biographies 71
Appendix: Robert Colinson and his Idea Rationaria 73
Index to authors 79
Index to titles 97
Addenda 106

LIST OF ILLUSTRATIONS

Malcolm: Waste Book (1718) xi, facing page 4
Fisher: Calligraphy (1772) xii, facing page 5
Halbert: List of subscribers (1789) xiii, facing page 12
Brodie: Day Book (1831) xiv, facing page 13
Robert Hamilton, LL.D., F.R.S.E. (1743 - 1829) xv, facing page 22
James McClelland, C.A. (Glasgow, 1799 - 1879) xvi, facing page 23
James Meston, C.A. (Aberdeen, 1821 - 1892) xvii, facing page 28
Sir John Mann, C.A. (Glasgow, 1864 - 1955) xviii, facing page 29
Colinson: Idea Rationaria, title page 72
Colinson: Profit and Loss Account (1683) 76 & 77

INTRODUCTION TO SECOND EDITION

This bibliography lists books and articles concerning accounting and related subjects in Scotland. It is divided into three parts: the first lists books published in Scotland, on accounting, book-keeping and commercial arithmetic, between 1683 and 1920; the second includes transcriptions and discussions of Scottish accounts before the early 1800s; the third deals with Scottish accounting history and includes, in section iii, a selection of biographical sketches concerning, mostly, accountants in practice before the beginning of the twentieth century. In part I keys to the various arithmetical and "question and answer" type texts have been excluded. In parts II and III a section, ii, listing selections of relevant periodical articles has been included.

The bibliography is arranged chronologically, parts I, III i and III ii by date of publication of the first or earliest known edition, part II by the date of commencement of the account, and part III iii by the date of the death of the subject. The items are numbered sequentially throughout and all references are made to the item number and not to the page number. A quick reference column to the dates is given in the right hand margin of each page. Alphabetical author and title indexes are given, title entries being made by the first word not an article. Sub-titles have been included.

Entries have been made according to the Anglo-American Cataloguing Rules 1967, with abbreviated locations for eleven Scottish and English libraries (see page x). A number of locations in other British and overseas libraries have been added, the names of these libraries being given in fuller form. A note of references made to an item in major works on accounting history is also given. A guide to the abbreviations used in the bibliography, to locations, references and journals, is given immediately prior to the bibliography (see page ix). For any items not originally individually examined by the compiler a note (Not seen) is given, together with a fuller source reference if needed. Only brief entries have been made for subsequent editions of items, and if no pagination is given it will be the same as in previous editions.

ABBREVIATIONS

General

ch.	chapter	n.p.	no printer given
cm.	centimetres	p.	page
cont.	continued	pub.	published
ed.	edition	REF.	reference
illus.	illustrated	Scott. Hist. Soc.	Scottish History Society
ll.	leaves	ser.	series
LOC.	location	v.	volume
n.d.	no date given		

Journals

Acc. The Accountant. 1874 -

Acc. Mag. The Accountant's Magazine. 1897 -

J. Acc. Journal of Accountancy. 1905 -

Loc. Gov. Fin. Local Government Finance. 1935 -

N.N.Q. or Scot. Antiq. Northern Notes and Queries, or, The Scottish Antiquary. 1886 - 1890.
continued as: Scot. Antiq. or N.N.Q.

Proc. Soc. Antiq. Scot. Proceedings of the Society of Antiquities of Scotland. 1851/1852 -

Scot. Antiq. or N.N.Q. The Scottish Antiquary or Northern Notes and Queries. 1891 - 1903.
continued as: Scot. Hist. Rev.

Scot. Hist. Rev. The Scottish Historical Review. 1904 -

Trans. C.A. Stud. Soc. Edin. Transactions of the Chartered Accountants' Students' Society of Edinburgh. 1886 - 1914.

Trans. Dum. & Gall. N.H. & Antiq. Soc. Transactions of the Dumfriesshire and Galloway Natural History and Antiquarian Society. 1862 -

Trans. East Loth. Antiq. & F.N. Soc. Transactions of the East Lothian Antiquarian and Field Naturalists Society. 1924/45 -

Trans. Gael. Soc. Inverness. Transactions of the Gaelic Society of Inverness. 1872 -

Trans. Hawick Arch. Soc. Transactions of the Hawick Archaeological Society. 1865 -

Locations

AUL Aberdeen University Library, Kings College.

BM* British Museum Library, now the National Reference Library.

E The Institute of Chartered Accountants in England and Wales, London.

EP Edinburgh Public Libraries, the Reference Library.

EUL Edinburgh University Library.

GP Glasgow Public Libraries, the Mitchell Library.

GUL Glasgow University Library.

L* British Library of Political and Economic Science, the Library of the London School of Economics, University of London.

NLS National Library of Scotland, Edinburgh.

SE The Institute of Chartered Accountants of Scotland, Edinburgh.

SG The Institute of Chartered Accountants of Scotland, Glasgow.

* locations have been taken from the respective catalogues of these libraries.

References

DM "Chapters in the history of bookkeeping, accountancy and commercial arithmetic" by David Murray, Glasgow, 1930. (Item 280)
numbers refer to page numbers of the text.

RB "History of accounting and accountants" by Richard Brown. Edinburgh, 1905. (Items 159 and 279)
b- bibliography, p. 343-360.

YET "Accounting in England and Scotland, 1543 - 1800" by B.S. Yamey, H.C. Edey and H.W. Thomson, London, 1963. (Item 285)
b- bibliography, p. 202-224
x - extracted. An alphabetical author index to the extracts is given in the introduction to the book.

PART I: BOOKS PUBLISHED IN SCOTLAND, 1683 - 1920

Part I is arranged chronologically by date of the first, or earliest located, Scottish edition.

1 COLINSON, Robert. 1683

Idea rationaria, or, The Perfect accomptant, necessary for all merchants and trafficquers, containing the true form of bookkeeping according to the Italian method ... Edinburgh: David Lindsay, James Kniblo, Josua van Solingen and John Colmar, 1683.

(8), (276)p. 31cm.

REF: DM-3,32,43,313; RB-b; YET-xb.

LOC: SE; EUL; GUL; E; NLS; BM.

The first Scottish work on bookkeeping. See appendix p. 73.

2 PATERSON, James. 1685

The Scots arithmetician, or, Arithmetick in all its parts... Edinburgh: Joshua van Solingen and John Colmar, 1685.

(14), 144p. 15cm.

REF: DM-8,312,314.

LOC: SE; GUL; NLS; BM.

------(another edition) Edinburgh: 1688.

LOC: SE.

The first work on commercial arithmetic published in Scotland.

3 HERIOT, Alexander. 1697

A Book containing tables for finding out the exchange of money and annualrents for days, months and years, with a further description of the various uses of the saids tables. Edinburgh: the heirs and successors of Andrew Anderson, 1697.

(20), 40p. 19cm.

REF: DM-3,43,315.

LOC: NLS; AUL; GUL.

Heriot was a teacher of bookkeeping in Edinburgh. He wrote, he claimed, so that "we should not be altogether beholden to Forreigners, as many times we are".

4 BROWN, George. 1700

An Account of the rotula arithmetica ... together with instructions how to use it. Edinburgh: Mathias Symson for the author, 1700.

88p. 13cm.

REF: -

LOC: EUL; GUL; NLS; Cambridge

See D.J. Bryden, "George Brown, Author of the Rotula", *Annals of Science*, v.28 (1972) p. 1-29. The rotula arithmetica was a very simple and not very successful calculating machine. The original model is in the National Museum of Antiquities of Scotland, Edinburgh.

5 BROWN, George 1700

A Specie book serving at one look, to turne any pure number (that is to say any number of unites, tens, hundreds or thousands, etc.) of any piece of silver current in this Kingdom, to pounds Scots or Sterling. (Edinburgh): (n.p.), 1700.

20p. (1 fold.) 11cm.

(Not seen)

REF: DM-13.

LOC: -

The only copy of this work known to Bryden, op.cit., is in the Royal Scottish Museum, Department of Technology.

6 BROWN, George. 1701

A Compendious but a compleat system of decimal arithmetick containing more exact rules for ordering infinites than any hitherto extant. Edinburgh: for the author, 1701.

68p. 10cm.

REF: -

LOC: SE; EUL; GUL; EP; NLS; BM; Leningrad Academy of Sciences.

"An extensive and prolix treatment of decimals" (Bryden, op. cit., p.20).

7 GREAT BRITAIN: Customs. 1707

Instructions for the collectors and other officers employ'd in Her Majesties' Customs, etc., in the north part of Great Britain with ... the regular methods of accompting. Edinburgh: the heirs and successors of Andrew Anderson, 1707.

32+78p. (9 fold.) 38cm.

REF: -

LOC: SE; EUL.

Detailed models are given of all necessary books of account. A manuscript note in the EUL copy attributes authorship to John Crookshanks, esq.

8 (SPENCE, David.) 1714

Arithmetick compendiz'd, or, A Short treatise of arithmetick ... by a member of the Society. Edinburgh: the heirs and successors of Andrew Anderson, 1714.

(8),87p. 16cm.

REF: DM-317.

LOC: SE; NLS; BM.

------with the addition of some tables of interest. Edinburgh: 1721.

viii,88p.

LOC: BM.

The author was Secretary to the Bank of Scotland.

9 NEWALL, W. 1715

The New Merchant's companion being a more exact, quick and easy way for making up of accompts ... Glasgow: Donald Govan, 1715.

(6),248p. 15cm.

REF: DM-331.

LOC: GUL; GP.

A ready reckoner, plus a list of the principal fairs in Scotland, England and Wales.

10 BROWN(E), George. 1717

Arithmetica infinita, or, The Accurate accomptant's best companion ... (?): for the author, 1717/18.

ii,150p. 10x13cm.

REF: DM-12.

LOC: SE; EUL; GUL; E; NLS; BM.

A ready reckoner. Bryden, op.cit., feels that this book was most probably published in London, though earlier sources assume Edinburgh.

11 DRUMMOND, John. 1718

The Accomptant's pocket companion: a manual instructing merchants, gentlemen of estates and others, to begin their books, carry on their business and make a ballance;.., Edinburgh: (n.p.), 1718.

21p. 19cm.

REF: DM-45, 317/8; YET-b.

LOC: SE; E; NLS; BM; L; Columbia.

Very brief. The reader is referred to "my Sett of Books, entitled, Merchant accompts made easy", but this was apparently never published.

12 LUNDIN, Robert. 1718

The Reason for accompting by debitor and creditor with general rules for attaining to that way of accompting. Edinburgh: (n.p.), 1718.

14(i.e.20)p. 23cm.

REF: DM-44,318; YET-b.

LOC: NLS; L.

-----The Fundamental principles and reasons of accompting by debitor and creditor ... 2nd.ed. corrected and enlarged. Edinburgh: (n.p.), 1736.

viii,32+(30)p. 26cm.

LOC: EUL.

Lundin was a teacher of bookkeeping and arithmetic in Edinburgh. In the introduction to the 2nd edition he hopes to "find no reasonable Person who will say that I teach according to Collinson, M'Ghie, M'Colm (see 1 above, 13 and 14 below) etc. their Method, or have composed an ignorant Omnigatherum from all or any of them" (p.iii). Unlike many later authors, he recommends "the Female Sex" to learn double entry bookkeeping: "it is very probable, that many Families who have lost their fortunes, might have preserved them, if the Ladies had known how to keep a regular Accompt" (p.iv).

13 MacGHIE, Alexander. 1718

The Principles of bookkeeping explain'd with the chief cases thereof stated and resolved, to which are annexed two setts of books of Fictitious trade, wherein the whole is reduced to practice. Edinburgh: James Watson for the author's relict, 1718.

(6),66+(108)p. 24cm.

REF: DM-44,317; RB-b; YET-xb.

LOC: SE; GUL; E; Columbia, N.Y.

The first of a series of 18th century Scottish authors, (MacGhie, Malcolm, Mair, Gordon, R. Hamilton) whose treatises "are all good in relation to their objective of giving instruction and advice methodically and clearly" (YET p.172, Yamey). More detailed than Colinson. MacGhie was a merchant and teacher of arithmetic and bookkeeping in Edinburgh.

Both Murray and Brown state that this is the second edition of a work published in 1715. No trace an earlier work has been found, and the 1718 copy gives no indication that it is a subsequent edition.

14 MALCOLM, Alexander. 1718

A New treatise of arithmetic and bookkeeping ... Edinburgh: John Mosman and William Brown for John Paton (bookseller), 1718.

(12),372p. 24cm.

REF: DM-44,317/8; RB-b; YET-b.

LOC: SE; EUL; GUL; E; NLS; BM; AUL; St Andrews; Oxford; Cambridge; Columbia.

Malcolm was a teacher of mathematics in Edinburgh and later in Aberdeen. He was also the author of A New System of Arithmetick, Theoretical and Practical (1730) and A Treatise of Bookkeeping (London, 1731. 2nd.ed. 1743). The latter is recommended by Yamey to business historians seeking contemporary guidance on 17th and 18th century accounting practice (T.C. Barker, R.H. Campbell, P. Mathias, Business History, Historical Association, (1960), p.35). In the 1718 book, Malcolm deliberately does not include " a tedious Collection of Questions and Answers, put upon every Case and Circumstance that may be supposed, and the most of them very trifling" (p.127) and states his preference for keeping "the Stock-Accompt clean of every Thing but what belonged to the last Inventary, for it is the proper Office of the Accompt of Profit and Loss to receive all the Encrease and Decrease of the Stock" (p.143).

15 SMITH, James. 1718

Tables of annualrent or simple interest of money at the rates of 4,4½,5,5½ and 6 per cent per annum from five shillings to 1000 pounds for 1...(to)..12 months with three tables of reduction of money ... with directions and examples. Edinburgh: by the successors of Andrew Anderson for the author, 1718.

(28)p. 15cm.

REF: DM-317.

LOC: NLS; Oxford.

16 HAMILTON, Robert. 1727

Rental accounts made easy, or, A Clear and distinct method by which persons of estates,... may ..see what they have received... and what is yet due ...Edinburgh: for the author, 1727.

22p. 1 plate (fold). 17cm.

REF: -

LOC: EP.

WASTE-BOOK.

	l.	s.	d.
Shipped aboard the *Swan* of *Kirkcaldy*, *David Fortune* Master, these following Goods, for *Rochel* consigned to *Daniel Stratton* my Factor there, to be disposed for my Account, *viz.* l.			
Impr. 168 Barrels of Herrings of my own cost : : 126			
It. 280 Yards white Plaiden received this Day from *Alexander Brigs* for ready Money : : : : : : } 7			
It. 40 Barrel of Beef, bought this Day from *James Montgomery*, payable in 1 Month : : : } 60			
193 : :			
Charges at Shipping paid, is : : 4 16 8			
Freight owing to the Owners of the Ship, : 10			
207 16 8	207	16	8
——— *Ditto* 22d, ———			
I have lent to *Thomas Speedwell* on Bottomry of his Ship the *Mary* of *Borrowstounness* 50 *l.* to be paid at her Arrival at *Lisbon*, to *Cornelius Mandoli* my Factor there, with 24 *l.* of Interest for my Risk, Total : : : : : :	74		
I have wagered against *John Ramsay*, that the *British* Parliament shall not be adjourned until the 1st of *July* next (if then) both of us consigned in the Hands of *John Blackadder*, my Consignation is	5		
——— *Ditto* 25th, ———			
Bought of Mr. *James Trustwell* 4 Packs of Wooll, Number and Weight as follows, *viz.* *Stone* *Pd.*			
No. 1. containing 18			
No. 2. containing 22 14			
No. 3. containing 30			
No. 4. containing 25 10			
Total gross 96 08			
3 allowed for Tare, which comes to near ½ *pd.* to 1 *Stone.*			
93 08 Neat Weight at 10 *s.* 7 *d. per* Stone, is 49 *l.* 09 *s.* 6 *d.* ½, whereof I have paid in Money : : : : 19 09 6½			
Given him 6 Barrels of Figs at 3 *per* Barrel *l.* 18			
The Remainder payable 1st *August* : 12			
49 09 6½	49	9	6½

I have

A page of the Waste Book from Alexander Malcolm:

A New treatise of arithmetick and bookkeeping ...

Edinburgh, 1718

(see item 14)

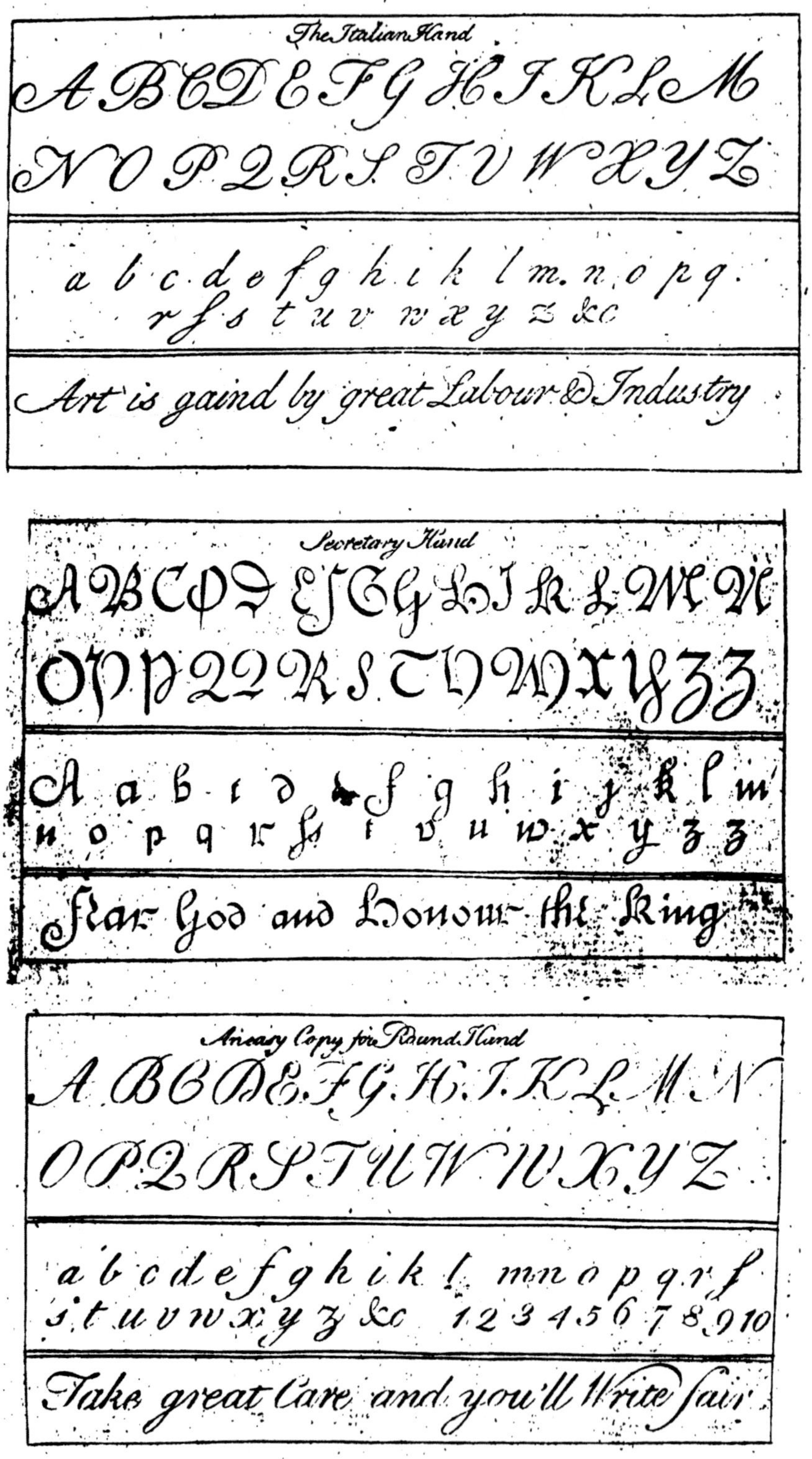

Calligraphy examples from George Fisher:
The Instructor, or, Young man's best companion ...
Edinburgh, 1763
(see item 30)

17 STEVENSON, William. 1732

A General discourse shewing the usefulness of the Italian method of bookkeeping and the practice of exchange. Edinburgh: R. Fleming and co., 1732.

(4),28p. 17cm.

REF: DM-46,319/21; YET-b.

LOC: GUL.

The text of a lecture delivered in St. Mary's Chapel, Niddry's Wynd, Edinburgh, on Monday 8th November, 1731. Stevenson states that lawyers are often "puzzled in carrying on their Clients Processes, by their not being thoroughly acquainted with Numbers, and the Nature of stating Accounts ... For which Reason they are frequently obliged to employ Accomptants to regulate the Accounts" (p.14). He also argues "that 'till a Man has so disposed his Concerns in this World, he cannot be said to be prepared for the other" (p.24).

18 HAMILTON, William. 1735

Bookkeeping new modelled, or, A Treatise of merchant's accounts according to the true Italian method of debitor and creditor ... Edinburgh: R. Fleming for the author, 1735.

(8),85(i.e.87)+(84)p. 22cm.

REF: DM-321/24; YET-b.

LOC: GUL; E; NLS.

Describes himself on the title page as M.M.P. which Murray suggests means Mathematical Master, Perth.

19 MAIR, John. 1736

Bookkeeping methodiz'd, or, A Methodical treatise of merchant-accompts, according to the Italian form ... Edinburgh: T. & W. Ruddimans, for the author, 1736; also another 1736 edition (248p.) Edinburgh: W. Sands, Brymer, A. Murray and J. Cochran.

xii,173+75p. 21cm.

REF: DM-48,324; RB-b; YET-xb.

LOC: SE; E; L; NLS; Columbia; Keele (Turner Collection); Buffalo & Erie County Public Library; Harvard.

------2nd.ed. Edinburgh: Sands, Brymer, Murray and Cochran, 1741.

xiv,250p. 21cm.

LOC: SE; GUL; NLS; BM; Univ. of California, Berkeley; Columbia Univ.; Library of Congress.

------3rd.ed. Edinburgh: 1749.

xiv,288p. 21cm.

LOC: SE; E; Columbia; Library of Congress; Univ. of California; Rutgers University.

------4th.ed. Edinburgh: 1752.

LOC: SE; E; L; Oxford; Canberra Univ.; Harvard; American Institute of CPAs; Madrid.

------5th.ed. Edinburgh: 1757.

xiv,416p.

LOC: AUL; E; NLS; BM; GUL; California; Columbia; Library of Congress; Harvard; Duke Univ.; Univ. of Florida; Virginia State Library, Richmond.

------6th.ed. Edinburgh: 1760.

LOC: GUL; E; BM; Univ. of Baltimore; Boston Public Lib.; Miami Univ.; Univ. of Pennsylvania; Folger Shakespeare Library.

19 MAIR, John. (cont.) 1736

Bookkeeping methodiz'd.

------7th.ed. Edinburgh: 1763.

xiv,416p. 22cm.

LOC: SE; SG; E; NLS; Oxford; Columbia; Chicago University; Paris (Bibl. Nat.); Yale; Univ. of Baltimore; Univ. of Virginia; Cornell.

------8th.ed. Edinburgh: 1765.

LOC: SE; E; Library of Congress; Universities of:- Baltimore, Chicago, Columbia, Harvard, Illinois, Virginia.

Mair's books, on mathematics, bookkeeping, Latin and geography, were deservedly bestsellers in Britain and Ireland. He was a graduate in Arts of St. Andrews University and teacher of mathematics and bookkeeping at Ayr Grammar School and Perth Academy. The 6th.edition (1760) of Methodiz'd was translated into Norwegian in 1775 and was the first text on bookkeeping published in Norway. The preface to Moderniz'd (item 37 below) explains that "as forms and fashions in accountantship as well as in other things, are in a perpetual flux, and continually changing, I resolved once more to turn my thoughts on this useful and important subject, with a view to expunge whatever might appear less modish or obsolete, and give the whole a higher degree of perfection, and consequently a better title to public approbation". See also item 309.7.

20 INNES, John. 1741

A Dissertation concerning the arithmetick of annuities. Edinburgh: R. Fleming and A. Alison, 1741.

24p. 25cm.

REF: -

LOC: SE; NLS.

21 WILSON, John. 1741

An Introduction to arithmetick ... together with the more necessary and useful rules in business ... Edinburgh: R. Drummond and Co., 1741.

xiv(ii),260p. 20cm.

REF: -

LOC: SE; GUL; NLS; BM; St Andrews; Oxford; Univ. College, London (Graves).

------2nd.ed. Ed. John Mair/Edinburgh: 1752.

xiv,312p.

LOC: NLS; GUL; St. Andrews; Univ. College, London; King's College, London.

22 COCKER, Edward revised by George FISHER 1749

Cocker's arithmetick ... 53rd.ed. carefully corrected and amended by George Fisher. Glasgow: John Hall, 1749.

(vi),183p. 16cm.

REF: -

LOC: SE; GUL; GP; Ann Arbor.

Cocker's book on arithmetic was the most famous of its time and was also revised by John Mair (item 23 below).

23 COCKER, Edward revised by John MAIR. 1751

Cocker's arithmetic, ... revised and corrected by John Mair. Edinburgh: Sands, Murray and Cochran, 1751.

(6),186p. 17cm.

REF: -

LOC: SE; EP; GUL; Chicago University.

-----(another edition) Edinburgh: 1760.
LOC: SE; GUL.

-----(another edition) Edinburgh: 1762.
LOC: GUL; NLS; BM; Ann Arbor; Urbana, Illinois.

----- A new edition. Edinburgh: 1765.
LOC: SE; GUL; NLS; London University (De Morgan Collection).

-----(another edition) Edinburgh: 1771.
LOC: GUL; Ann Arbor; Chicago University.

-----(another edition) Edinburgh: 1780.
LOC: St Andrews.

-----(another edition) Glasgow: 1787.
LOC: SE; EUL; GUL; Ann Arbor.

24 FISHER, George. 1756

Arithmetic in the most plainest and most concise methods hitherto extant with new improvements for dispatch of business ... 10th.ed. Glasgow: John Bryce and David Paterson for Charles Hutcheson (bookseller), 1756.

xii,312p. 18cm.

REF: -

LOC: GP.

-----12th.ed. Glasgow: 1761.
LOC: GUL.

-----A new edition. Glasgow: 1767.
LOC: SE.

-----(another edition) Glasgow: 1772.
LOC: GUL; GP.

-----(another edition) Glasgow: 1774.
LOC: GUL.

-----(another edition) Glasgow: 1777.
LOC: GUL.

-----(another edition) Paisley: 1780.
(Not seen)
LOC: GP.

-----(another edition) (London and) Glasgow: Ayr: 1795.

The earliest located edition is the 2nd., London, 1726, at Christchurch, Oxford.

25 STEVENSON, William. 1756

A Serious advice to tradesmen. Shewing them the inconveniencies they lye under and needless expence they are put to by not learning bookkeeping ... Edinburgh: R. Fleming, 1756.

(4),29p. 18cm.

REF: RB-b; YET-b.

LOC: SE.

Not a text book. Quotes John Locke's recommendation of book-keeping "as a science well becoming every Gentleman" (for the full text see J.L. Axtell, The Educational Writings of John Locke, C.U.P. (1968) p.319 et seq.) and observes that "some of the old authors are the best, and most substantial, as having been either Traders themselves, or taken their books from those of real Trade; though our new ones make their productions more elaborate, and fill them with Mathematical Learning, heaping numbers of problems and theorems, which might be said in few words, and made more intelligible to learners, in a plain and simple narrative" (pp.11-12).

YET include in their bibliography a book by Stevenson entitled "An Advice to tradesmen to learn bookkeeping", Edinburgh, 1756. No location is given, and no other reference to the work has been found. It would appear to be an abbreviated title of this item.

26 CRAIGHEAD, William. 1757

Arithmetic in all its parts, vulgar and decimal ... Dundee: Henry Galbraith and co., 1757.

(8),564p. 17cm.

REF: -

LOC: Dundee Public Library.

------(another edition) Dundee: 1760.

LOC: SE; GUL.

------(another edition) Edinburgh: 1798.

LOC: Dundee Public Library; NLS.

Probably the first extant book printed in Dundee. The author, a schoolmaster in Monifieth, also wrote The Merchants Companion, after a new method. Dundee: H. Galbraith and co., 1761 (copy in Dundee Public Library).

27 WEBSTER, William. 1758

Essays on bookkeeping ... To which is added a large appendix containing a variety of specimens in company accounts ... and a method of keeping accompts proper for shop-keepers or retailers, by a teacher of bookkeeping. Glasgow: for John Orr, 1758.

xii,216p. 18cm.

REF: DM-39,336/7; YET-b.

LOC: GUL; GP; E; Columbia.

Originally published in London, 1719, without the appendix.

28 LEYBOURN, William. 1761

Panarithmologia, or, The Traders' sure guide, containing tables ... adapted to the use of merchants, mercers, bankers, ... 13th.ed. Glasgow: J. Bryce and A. McLean, jr., for John Orr, 1761.

28 LEYBOURN, William.(cont.) 1761

Panarithmologia ...

239p. 11cm.

REF: DM-332.

LOC: NLS; GUL.

-----The Ready reckoner. (2nd.(Scottish)edition). Glasgow: A. Adams, 1776.

LOC: GUL.

(Not seen, ref.DM-332)

A ready reckoner. Originally published in London in 1693.

29 STEVENSON, William. 1762

Book-keeping by double entry reduced in its theory to one simple rule. Edinburgh: R. Stirling, 1762.

vi,202p. 38cm.

REF: DM-45; YET-b.

LOC: SE; EUL; E; NLS; BM; Columbia.

Title page states that the author had been "some time Merchant in Rotterdam" and was "present Teacher of book-keeping, Authorised by Act of Council of the City of Edinburgh." There is a list of subscribers: these include an "accomptant" and three "accomptants of excise".

30 FISHER, George. 1762

The Instructor, or, Young man's best companion containing ... merchant accounts and a short and easy method of shop and book-keeping ... 16th.ed. Edinburgh: Gavin Alston, 1762.

iv,370p. 18cm.

REF: RB-b; YET-b.

LOC: GUL; Newcastle Univ. Lib.

-----(another edition) Edinburgh: 1763.

xii,384p. 18cm.

LOC: NLS; Oxford.

------21st.ed. Edinburgh: 1767.

LOC: EUL; NLS; Urbana; Dept. of Science and Education, London.

------22nd.ed. Edinburgh: 1768.

LOC: EUL; Amer. Phil. Soc., Philadelphia.

------23rd.ed. Edinburgh: 1771.

LOC: Columbia.

-----A new edition. Edinburgh: 1772.

LOC: SE; National Library of Wales.

------22nd.edition (numeration fits London sequence). Edinburgh: 1778.

LOC: Boston Athenaeum.

------(another edition). Edinburgh: 1780.

LOC: NLS.

------(a new edition). Edinburgh: 1784.

------(new edition) Glasgow: 1786.

LOC: Library of Congress; Oberlin College.

------A new edition, carefully corrected. Glasgow: 1796.

xii,396p.

LOC: BM.

30 FISHER, George. (cont.) 1762

The Instructor ...

——(another edition) Edinburgh: 1799.
LOC: NLS.

——(another edition) Edinburgh: 1840.
LOC: GUL.

——(another edition) Edinburgh: 1841.
(Not seen).

A pocket book which includes sections on commercial arithmetic and double entry bookkeeping.

David Murray (p.308) states that George Fisher was a pseudonym for Mrs Slack, but later research has shown this to be incorrect: L.C. Karpinski, "The Elusive George Fisher 'Accomptant' - Writer or Editor of Three Popular Arithmetics", Scripta Mathematica, 1935 p.337-9. Karpinski also draws attention to the success of an American edition of the book published by Benjamin Franklin and David Hall in Philadelphia in 1748.

There is a description of the "Young man's best companion" in a one-page article by K. Quester, The Accountant, 7 December, 1940 p.430.

In 1816 an attorney was sentenced to seven year's transportation at the Gloucester Spring Assizes for administering an unlawful oath using a copy of this book: R. v. Brodribb, 6 Car. & P.571.

31 GORDON, William. 1763

The Universal accountant and complete merchant, in two volumes. Edinburgh: A. Donaldson and J. Reid for Alex. Donaldson, 1763-5.
2v. (x,408; vi,466)p. 22cm.
REF: DM-34; YET-xb; RB-b.
LOC: EUL; NLS; BM; L; Library of Congress: Philadelphia Lib. Co.

——2nd.ed. Edinburgh: 1765.
LOC: E; St Andrews (1st.v. only); Paris; Univ. Coll., London (Graves).

——3rd.ed. Edinburgh: 1770.
LOC: SE (2nd. v. only); GUL; Royal Society; Paris.

——4th.ed. Edinburgh: 1777.
2v. (xii,462; vi,466)p. 20cm.

——5th.ed. Edinburgh: 1787.
LOC:-
(Not seen. Source, YET bibliography).

The first volume includes an "Essay on the education of a young gentleman intended for the counting-house" and four parts: The elements of arithmetic; Of fractions; The elements of algebra; The application of arithmetic to the business of the merchant, the banker, customhouse, insurance office, etc. (including stock-jobbing: "the business ... is generally carried on by the brokers, who ... make their fortunes by bubbling their clients, and have entered into a kind of conspiracy to keep the method of trading in the stocks a mystery to every one but themselves" (4th.ed. v.1,p.241)). The second volume is prefaced by a Dissertation on the business of the counting house and is also divided into four parts: The elements of mercantile accountantship; Mercantile accountantship reduced to practice, in various specimens of books, connected and digested as in real trade; Of bills of exchange and promissory notes; A brief view of the British customs.

31 GORDON, William (cont.) 1763

The Universal accountant ...

The first arithmetic by an American author, Chauncy Lee's American Accomptant, (Lansingburgh, N.Y., 1797) to contain a section on double entry, contained 297 pages of which 42 were devoted to "a compendium of the Italian mode of bookkeeping agreeable to Gordon's system of accomptantship": H.C. Bentley and R.S. Leonard, Bibliography of Works on Accounting by American Authors (1934), 2v., v.1., p.iv.

32 HILL, John. 1764

Arithmetic, both in theory and practice ... Edinburgh: John Gray and Gavin Alston, 1764.

(Not seen).

REF:

LOC: St Andrews.

-----13th.ed. Edinburgh: 1765.

LOC: SE; GUL; St Andrews.

-----15th.ed. Edinburgh: 1777.

LOC: GUL; NLS.

-----16th.ed. Edinburgh: 1788.

(Not seen).

Originally published in London, 1713.

33 GORDON, William. 1766

The General counting-house and man of business ... Edinburgh: for A. Donaldson, 1766.

vi, 487p. 21cm.

REF: RB-b; YET-b.

LOC: SE; EUL; GUL; E; NLS; BM.

-----2nd.ed. Edinburgh: 1770.

LOC: E; Oxford.

Gordon, Dobson and Scruton carried on together, for some time, a mercantile academy in Glasgow (see also items 31, 36 and 41).

Almost identical with v.2 of item 31 above, but excludes the brief view of the British customs, and includes material on the "West-India Counting-house", and accounting for retailers, gentlemen, chamberlains and farmers.

Included among the subsidiary books mentioned in this work are a Book of Wares "kept in order to know at all times by inspection, what merchandises are lodged in the warehouse, what are taken out of it, and what remains on hand, in which the quantity, quality and volume is particularly expressed" and a Book of Workmen, "particularly used by those traders who have manufactures, and is kept in the way of Dr and Cr, there being an account for every workman that is employed. On the Debtor-side are expressed the materials which are given to them for manufacturing, and on the Creditor-side the work which they bring home when manufactured" (pp.15-16). It is recommended that goods unsold be stated at prime cost (pp.40,425) but rum on hand is valued at market in the specimen accounts (pp.75,243).

34 MAIR, John. 1766

Arithmetic, rational and practical ... consisting of three parts, I: Vulgar arithmetic, II: Decimal arithmetic, III: Practical arithmetic. Edinburgh: Sands, Murray and Cochran for A. Kincaid and J. Bell, 1766.

2v. (xii,474; iv,356+(4 fold.))p. 18cm.

REF: -

LOC: EUL; NLS; AUL; BM; St. Andrews; Cambridge; Univ. Coll., London.

-----(2nd.ed.) Edinburgh: 1772.

LOC: GUL.

-----(3rd.ed.) Edinburgh: 1777.

xii,615p.

LOC: NLS; St. Andrews; Perth Public Library; Perth Academy; Paris.

-----(4th.ed.) Edinburgh: 1786.

LOC: GUL; EUL; Newcastle Univ. Lib.

-----5th.ed. Edinburgh: 1794.

(in 1 v.) xii,615+4(fold)p. 22cm.

LOC: EUL; NLS; GUL; Perth Academy.

-----6th.ed. Edinburgh: 1799.

LOC: EP; Perth Public Library; St. Andrews; Oxford.

35 THOMSON, John. 1768

Tables of interest at 3,4,4½ and 5 per cent from £1 to £10,000 and 1 day to 365 in a regular procession of single days. Edinburgh: J. Kincaid and J. Bell, 1768.

vi,400p. 17cm.

REF: DM-334.

LOC: NLS; BM; GP; GUL.

-----(another edition) Edinburgh: 1766.

LOC: GUL; EUL; Newcastle University.

-----3rd.ed. Edinburgh: 1783.

-----4th.ed. Edinburgh: 1786.

LOC: NLS; BM; Leeds Univ.; Oxford; Cambridge (Trinity Coll.); Paris.

-----5th.ed. Edinburgh: 1788.

vi,531p. 17cm.

LOC: BM; NLS.

-----6th.ed. Edinburgh: 1794.

LOC: EP; BM; AUL.

-----7th.ed. Edinburgh: 1804.

LOC: SE; EUL.

-----(reissue of 7th.ed.) Edinburgh: 1805.

LOC: E; Dundee Public Library; Guildhall, London.

LIST OF SUBSCRIBERS.

A

LIEUT. Richard Adderton, Ayr
Meſſ. Adam Anderſon, farmer do
James Anderſon, ſchoolmaſter, Dunlop
Robert Allan, engineer, Catrine
John Andrew, Monkton
William Andrew, maſon, Tarbolton
William Andrew, farmer at Troon
James Andrew, ſchoolmaſter, Paiſley
Andrew Aird, wright do

B

John Ballantine, Eſq; provoſt of Ayr
Meſſ. John Boſwell, writer do
Thomas Boyd, - do
James Baird, merchant do
Walter Bain, millwright, Leven printfield
Alexander Brown, Cordale
George Burns, maſon in Auchinleck
James Brown, Berryhill do
James Boyman, wright do
William Brown, merchant, Mauchline
Alexander Blair, Glaſgow—2 copies
John Brown, wright do
James Begg, maſon in Sorn
Robert Burns of Parnaſſus
William Brown, wright, Lainſhaw-milne
Thomas Brown, merchant, Stewarton
William Bell, ſen. ſchoolmaſter, Paiſley
David Brodie, do. Quarrelton
William Brown, copperſmith, Bridge-of-Johnſton

Meſſ.

Robert Burns, the poet, was one of the subscribers to William Halbert: The Practical figurer, or, An Improved system of Arithmetic ... Paisley, 1789 (see item 44)

Page in Journal.	PAISLEY, 1st JUNE 1830, P. M.	£	S.	D.
1	*Simon Sober & Company*, this afternoon, (in order to carry on their business) have taken a house, shop, stable, and shade, for three months, from Charles Careful, for which they are to pay £3 10/ at the end of each calendar month.			
	2.			
1	Received from Simon Sober to account of stock	25	0	0
1	Received from George Greedy to account of stock, 100 bolls potatoes, @ 9/6 ⅌ boll,	47	10	0
	3.			
1	Thomas Tippler has advanced, this date, to account of stock, 100 pints whisky, @ 4/6 ⅌ pint,	22	10	0
	4.			
1	Sold William White 20 bolls potatoes, @ 9/7 ⅌ boll, - - - -	9	11	8
	5.			
1	Sold for ready money 80 bolls potatoes @ 9/6½	38	3	4
	7.			
1	Sold 40 pints whisky to Barnard Black @ 5/	10	0	0
	8.			
1	Received from William White in part -	6	0	0
2	George Greedy has paid in, to account of stock, Hugh Humdrum's promissory note of 1st June, at two months, for £7 10 0 Off, 64 days' discount at 5 ⅌ cent. 0 1 4	7	8	8
	9.			
2	Thomas Tippler has transferred a debt due to him by Peter Pennyless, which is taken to account of stock paid in by him; *he*, Thomas Tippler, agreeing to ensure the debt, and to be paid in two weeks from this date—amount thereof - -	6	5	0
	10.			
2	George Greedy has advanced this day to account of stock 2 barrels of herrings @ 29/ ⅌ barrel	2	18	0
	14.			
2	Thomas Tippler has brought to account of stock 30 pints Highland whisky @ 5/ £7 10 0 and furnished a horse valued at - 8 15 0 and a saddle worth - - - 1 5 0	17	10	0

Page in Journal.	PAISLEY, 15th JUNE 1830.	£	S.	D.
2	Mr. Lawrence Lookabout, Excise Officer, having got information that the Highland whisky paid in by Thomas Tippler, as part of stock, was smuggled, therefore has seized the whole, in consequence thereof the £7 10/ is placed to Thomas Tippler's debit - - - - - - -	7	10	0
2	*Simon Sober* and *George Greedy* having suspicion of their other Partner, have examined the remaining 60 pints of whisky unsold, and find a deficiency of 8 pints @ 4/6 ⅌ pint; they therefore have placed the amount to Thomas Tippler's debit, *he* having all along had the sole management of the whisky department - - - - - -	1	16	0
	16.			
3	Sold Charles Catchpenny 42 pints whisky @ 5/ - - £10 10 0 And to Daniel Drouthy 10 pints do. @ 4/10 - 2 8 4 52	12	18	4
	17.			
3	Received from *Simon Sober* to account of stock	40	0	0
	18.			
3	The horse proving lame, has been sold to a Tanner for 15/, and the saddle not being needed, have sold it for 22/, both ready money - £1 17 0 which causes a loss on the transaction of 8 3 0	10	0	0
	24.			
3	Bought, for ready money, 20 gilt-framed looking-glasses, @ 21/ each - - -	21	0	0
	26.			
3	Peter Pennyless being seized with the palsy, is sent to an almshouse, and Thomas Tippler not being able to pay the sum for which he is security, therefore it is resolved by the other Partners to place the sum of £6 5/ to his debit - - -	6	5	0
3	Bought, for ready money, 48 framed prints @ 10/ each - - - - -	24	0	0
	28.			
3	Lent Nathaniel Needful for 10 days, @ 7½ ⅌ cent.	50	0	0

An extract from the Day-Book in David Brodie: A Short set of bookkeeping by double entry ... Paisley, 1831 (see item 79)

36 GORDON, William and DOBSON, Robert. 1771

The Elements, analysis and practice of arithmetic vulgar, decimal and duodecimal in all parts of modern business, mercantile or mechanical ... Glasgow: Robert Urie for the authors, 1771.

xiv,344p. 23cm.

REF: DM-35.

LOC: GUL; GP; Strathclyde University.

-----2nd.ed. Revised, corrected and enlarged by W. Gordon, Glasgow: A. Adam for Morrison and McCullum, 1775.

xiv,368p. 21cm.

LOC: GUL.

37 MAIR, John. 1773

Bookkeeping moderniz'd, or, Merchant-accounts by double entry, according to the Italian form ... Edinburgh: for A. Kincaid, W. Creech and J. Bell, 1773.

xii,620p. 21cm.

REF: DM-325; RB-b; YET-b.

LOC: SE; EUL; E; NLS; BM; Cambridge; Guildhall, London; Duke Univ.; Harvard; Yale; Universities of:- California, Illinois, Minnesota.

-----2nd.ed. Edinburgh: 1778.

LOC: SE; E; Univ. Coll., London; RIBA.

-----3rd.ed. Edinburgh: 1784.

LOC: SE; SG; E; Harvard; Univ. of Pennsylvania; Philadelphia Library Co.

-----4th.ed. Edinburgh: 1786.

LOC: SE; GUL; E; Princeton; Univ. of Baltimore.

-----5th.ed. Edinburgh: 1789.

LOC: SE; E; NLS; Harvard; Columbia; Duke Univ.; Boston Public Lib.; Univ. of Baltimore.

-----6th.ed. Edinburgh: 1793.

LOC: SE; E; Columbia; Chicago University; Paris; American Inst. of CPAs; Boston Public Lib.; Univ. of Baltimore; Univ. of Kentucky.

-----7th.ed. Edinburgh: 1797.

LOC: E; Columbia; Harvard; H.E. Huntingdon Lib., San Marino.

-----8th.ed. Edinburgh: 1800.

LOC: SE; E; NLS; Library of Congress; Boston Public Lib., Columbia; Harvard; Univ. of Baltimore; Univ. of California; New York Public Lib.; Yale.

-----9th.ed. Edinburgh: 1807.

LOC: SE; E; BM; Harvard; Yale; Univ. of Baltimore (variant).

Both Murray and Brown refer to the first edition as being published in 1768, but no copy of this date has been located. See items 19 and 309.7.

38 PERRY, William. 1774

The Man of business and gentleman's assistant, containing a treatise of practical arithmetic ... and bookkeeping by single and double entry ... Edinburgh: David Willison for the author, 1774.

xiv,466p. 4 plates(fold). 22cm.

REF: DM-49; RB-b; YET-b.

LOC: E; NLS; BM; EUL; Cambridge; Boston Athenaeum.

38 PERRY, William. (cont.) 1774

The Man of business ...

-----3rd.ed. Edinburgh: 1777.
LOC: EUL; E; NLS; BM; SE; Cambridge.

Perry was Master of the Academy at Kelso. There is a list of subscribers.

39 LAURIE, John. 1776

Tables of simple and compound interest calculated to ascertain the amount and present worth of Principal sums and annuities with their comparative values, whether interest and annuities be payable yearly or half-yearly. With explanation and examples. To which are subjoined a few remarks in which Dr. Price's observations on reversionary payments, etc. ... are clearly proven to be erroneous. Edinburgh: for the author, 1776.

viii,223p. 22cm.
REF: -
LOC: EUL; AUL; BM; GUL; E; Newcastle Univ. Lib.

Laurie was a teacher of mathematics in Edinburgh.

40 HAMILTON, Robert. 1777

An Introduction to merchandise ... Edinburgh: (n.p.), 1777.
2v. (vi,356; iv,364)p. 22cm.
REF: DM-49; RB-b; YET-xb.
LOC: EUL; BM; L; GUL; AUL; NLS.

------2nd.ed. Edinburgh: 1788.
(in 1 v.) viii,563p. 22cm.
LOC: SE; E; NLS; BM; Univ. Coll., London; Mathematics Assoc., Leicester Univ.

------3rd.ed. Edinburgh: 1797.
viii,571p. 22cm.
LOC: EUL; E; NLS; BM; AUL; St. Andrews; Paris.

------4th.ed. Edinburgh: 1799.
LOC: SE; E.

------5th.ed. Edinburgh: 1802.
LOC: SE; E; NLS; AUL.

------Revised by Elias Johnston. Edinburgh: 1820.
xiv,563p. 23cm.
LOC: SE; EUL; GUL; E; NLS; BM; AUL; Aberdeen Public Library.

Robert Hamilton, LL.D., F.R.S.E. (1743-1829) is the most interesting of the early Scottish writers on accounting. "In many ways (Hamilton's) has the most modern appearance of all the early books" (YET p.173). He was born in Edinburgh, the eighth son of a bookseller and publisher, and grandson of a principal of the University. After spending some time with William Hogg and Son, bankers, and as a partner in a paper mill, Hamilton became Rector of Perth Academy (1769) and whilst there wrote the first edition of Merchandise. He became professor of natural philosophy in the Marischal College, Aberdeen in 1779, moving later to the chair of mathematics. He became well known after the publication of his Inquiry concerning the Rise, Progress, Redemption, Present State and Management, of the National Debt of Great

40 HAMILTON, Robert. (cont.) 1777

An Introduction to merchandise ...

Britain and Ireland (Edinburgh, 1st.ed. 1813; 3rd.ed. 1818 reprinted in J.R. McCulloch, editor, A Select Collection of Scarce and Valuable Tracts and other Publications on the National Debt and Sinking Fund, London, 1857, reprinted by Augustus M. Kelley, New York, 1966). To this work he owes entries in the Dictionary of National Biography and Chambers' Biographical Dictionary of Eminent Scotsmen.

Merchandise is divided into six parts: arithmetic; algebra (including chapters on "doctrine of chances" and "annuities for lives"); bills, invoices, accompts, monies, weights and measures; Italian book-keeping; practical book-keeping; state and laws of trade (including some paragraphs on "stock-jobbing").

Merchants are recommended, "before balancing ... to take an exact inventory of the goods on hand, as far as can be done; and affix a moderate value to each article, according to the current price at the time: such a value as the owner would be willing at present to buy it for. It is much more proper to value the goods on hand in conformity to the current prices, than at prime cost: For the design of affixing any value is to point out the gain or loss; and the gain is in reality obtained so soon as the prices rise, or the loss suffered so soon as they fall" (2nd.ed., p.285). Artificers and manufacturers are recommended to keep a book of materials, a book of work and a book of wages; if a manufacturer "has an opportunity of beginning or desisting at any stage of the manufacture, his books should exhibit the gain or loss on each operation separately" (2nd.ed. p.487-8). (See item 295.1)

41 SCRUTON, James. 1777

The Practical counting-house, or, Calculation and accountantship ... Glasgow: for James Duncan, 1777.

viii,528p. 21cm.

REF: DM-338; RB-b; YET-b.

LOC: SE; GUL; E; L.

The most interesting part of this book is the Appendix "containing Precedents of Writing, English and Scots, proper for every regular Counting house; and a Book of Rates, Exhibiting, at one view, the Duty and Drawback upon every Commodity the British Merchant Exports or Imports, with a Summary of the Laws Respecting the same." The precedents follow Mair (19 and 37 above) very closely. Scruton was a teacher in Glasgow (see 33 above).

41.1 SCOTT, William. 1782

A New system of practical arithmetic for the use of schools and men of business. Edinburgh: C. Elliot, 1782.

vii,245p.8vo.

REF: -

LOC: NLS.

42 THOMSON, John. 1784

The Universal calculator, or, The Merchant's, tradesman's and family's assistant ... Edinburgh: Creech and Elliot, 1784.

xii,252p. 17cm.

REF: DM-332/3.

LOC: NLS; BM.

-----A new edition. Edinburgh: 1793.

LOC: E; NLS.

42 THOMSON, John. (cont.) 1784

The Universal calculator ...

-----(another edition) Edinburgh: 1798.
LOC: BM.

-----A new edition carefully corrected. Edinburgh: 1805.
LOC: SE; E; AUL; Oxford; Newcastle Univ. Lib.

Ready reckoner plus simple interest tables. Author is described on the title page as an "accomptant in Edinburgh".

43 SMITH, Thomas. 1785

Tables of interest for the use of bankers and others. Edinburgh: for the author, 1785.

vi,111p. 18cm.

REF: -
LOC: AUL; NLS; BM.

44 HALBERT, William. 1789

The Practical figurer, or, An Improved system of arithmetic ... Paisley: John Neilson, 1789.

298p. 23cm.

REF: DM-348/9.
LOC: EUL; GUL; GP; BM.

There is a ten page list of subscribers (with occupations), including "Robert Burns of Parnassus", the poet.

45 MORISON, John. 1789

Tables of interest at 3,4,4½ and 5 per cent from £1 to £10,000 in a regular succession of days from 1 to 365 ... Edinburgh: for William Creech, 1789.

vi,598p. 22cm.

REF: -
LOC: GUL; NLS; BM; Cambridge.

-----(another edition) Edinburgh: 1790.
LOC: SE; NLS.

46 YOUNG, David. 1790

The Farmer's account-book of expenditure and produce for each day, month and year ... Edinburgh: for the author, (1790).

74p. 43cm.

REF: DM-49; YET-b.
LOC: GUL.

47 MELROSE, A. 1791

Concise system of practical arithmetic ... Part I containing the fundamental rules and their application to the purposes of mercantile calculations. Edinburgh: 1791.

(Not seen; source B.M. catalogue)

REF: DM-328.
LOC: BM; AUL; GUL.

-----(another edition) Revised, corrected and greatly enlarged by A. Ingram. Edinburgh: 1812.
LOC: NLS; BM.

47 MELROSE, A. (cont.) 1791

Concise system of practical arithmetic ...

-----(another edition). Edinburgh: (1815).
LOC: GUL; London University Library.

-----(another edition) Revised, corrected and greatly enlarged, with tables of the monies, weights and measures now used in Great Britain and Ireland ... by William Stenhouse. Edinburgh: 1820.
vii,156p. 14cm.
LOC: GUL; BM.

-----8th.ed. Edinburgh: c.1830.
LOC: AUL.

-----12th.ed. Edinburgh: 1834.

-----15th.ed. Edinburgh: 1837.
LOC: St. Andrews.

-----18th.ed. Edinburgh: 1839.

-----20th.ed. Edinburgh: 1843.

-----22nd.ed. Edinburgh: 1846.

-----26th.ed. ... greatly enlarged by A. Ingram and J. Trotter, Edinburgh: 1853.
LOC: BM.

-----28th.ed. Edinburgh: 1854.
LOC: Library of Congress.

-----33rd.ed. Edinburgh: 1859.
LOC: St. Andrews.

-----37th.ed. Edinburgh: 1865.
LOC: BM; NLS; Oxford; Cambridge.

-----38th.ed. Edinburgh: 1866.
LOC: BM; NLS; Oxford; Cambridge.

-----41st.ed. Edinburgh: 1873.
LOC: BM.

-----42nd.ed. Edinburgh: 1874.
LOC: BM.

-----43rd.ed. Edinburgh: 1877.
LOC: BM.

-----44th.ed. Rearranged, improved and enlarged by A. Trotter. Edinburgh: 1881.
LOC: NLS; BM; St. Andrews; Oxford.

48 HAMILTON, Robert. 1796

A Short system of arithmetic and bookkeeping with a supplement containing answers to the arithmetical questions. 2nd.ed. Edinburgh: James Hunter, Bell and Bradfute ... , 1796.
xii,273p. 18cm.
REF: YET-b.
LOC: E.

48 HAMILTON, Robert. (cont.) 1796

A Short system of arithmetic ...

-----3rd.ed. Edinburgh: 1798.
LOC: NLS; BM; AUL.

-----5th.ed. Edinburgh: 1802.
LOC: E; BM.

-----7th.ed. Edinburgh: 1810.
LOC: AUL.

-----8th.ed. Edinburgh: 1815.
LOC: Aberdeen Public Library.

-----(another edition) Aberdeen: 1826.
LOC: Aberdeen Public Library.

First published in London, 1788.

An abridgement of An Introduction to Merchandise (item 40 above) but with new exercises.

49 BUCHANAN, Colin. 1798

The Writingmaster and accountant's assistant ... Glasgow: R. Chapman for the author, 1798.

80p. 23 plates. 27cm.
REF: DM-51; RB-b; YET-b.
LOC: SE; BM.

-----(another edition) Glasgow: 1800.
ii,(25 11)+41p. 25cm.
LOC: SE.

A commercial arithmetic, including some material on compound interest and annuities.

50 MORRISON, James. 1801

The Accomptant's guide. A new system of arithmetic for men of business, academies and schools. Glasgow: Niven, Napier and Khull for the author, 1801.

viii, 215p. 22cm.
REF: DM-12.
LOC: GP; NLS.

-----2nd.ed. with an appendix containing artificer's measuring ... Glasgow: 1806.
xii,306p. 22cm.
LOC: GUL; BM; GP; SE; St. Andrews.

-----4th.ed. Glasgow: 1808.
LOC: GUL.

51 MORRISON, James. 1803

A Complete treatise on practical bookkeeping, in which the elementary principles of every branch of the science are clearly explained and the most approved forms of the practice of the first

51 MORRISON, James. (cont.) 1803

A Complete treatise on practical bookkeeping, ... counting houses correctly exhibited in various specimens of books ... Edinburgh: 1803.

(Not seen)

REF: DM-43.

LOC: -

-----2nd.ed. with an appendix of exchange ... Edinburgh: 1810.

x,420p. 27cm.

LOC: NLS.

-----3rd.ed. Edinburgh: Oliver and Boyd, 1828.

xliv,422p. 24.5cm.

Morrison was Master of the Mercantile Academy, Glasgow. The chapter "Of Balancing the Books" repeats, without acknowledgement, Hamilton's (item 40 above) views on the valuation of goods on hand. Morrison's book is prefaced by a number of testimonials in favour, including one by Hamilton.

52 HUTTON, Charles revised by Alexander INGRAM. 1804

A Complete treatise on practical arithmetic and bookkeeping both by single and double entry, adapted to the use of schools, ... A new edition, corrected and enlarged by Alexander Ingram. Edinburgh: G. & J. Ross, 1804.

viii,259p. 18cm.

REF: YET-b.

LOC: E; GP; NLS.

-----(another edition) Edinburgh: 1805.

LOC: GUL; E.

-----(another edition) Edinburgh: 1807.

LOC: GUL; St. Andrews; London University (De Morgan).

-----A new edition. Hawick: 1810.

LOC: Manchester Public Library.

-----A new edition. Hawick: 1811.

LOC: E; NLS; BM; London University.

-----New edition adapted to the imperial standards of weights. Edinburgh: 1828.

LOC: BM; Oxford; Cambridge.

-----(another edition) Edinburgh: 1830.

LOC: Newcastle Univ. Lib.

-----(another edition) Edinburgh: 1837.

LOC: London Univ.

-----(another edition) Edinburgh: 1840.

LOC: E.

-----(another edition) Edinburgh: 1858.

LOC: E.

53 BUTTERWORTH & SON (publishers). 1805

Butterworth's young arithmeticians instructor ...
Edinburgh: Butterworth and son, 1805.
25 ll. 25cm.
REF: -
LOC: SE; GP.

54 BUCHANAN, Colin. 1806

Practical book-keeping being an attempt to assimilate the methods of the school to the practice of the counting house; ...
Edinburgh: James Muirhead for the author, 1806.
x,210p. 22cm.
REF: YET-b.
LOC: SE; GP.

Contains inter alia six sets of books "posted and balanced after the plainest and shortest methods" including one for a muslin manufacturer. Buchanan was a teacher in Greenock and the author of a book on arithmetic (item 49 above).

55 STENHOUSE, William. 1806

Tables of simple interest and of commission, brokerage and exchange ... Edinburgh: Alex. Smellie, 1806.
xviii,511p. 23cm.
REF: -
LOC: SE; NLS; BM.

There is a critical discussion in the Introduction of previous books of tables.

56 LORRAIN, William. 1807

Bookkeeping by double entry ... to which is added ... a course of bookkeeping by single entry. Hawick: Robert Armstrong, 1807.
viii,361p. 22cm.
REF: DM-339.
LOC: SE; BM.

A school textbook, including double entry for the use of the "schoolboy" and single entry for the use of "young ladies". The latter occupies pp.327-361 and consists of a day-book and a ledger with personal accounts only. The Preface promises the later issue of an Abridgement but this was apparently never published. Lorrain (1772-1842), a schoolmaster in Jedburgh, graduated M.A. (1797) and LL.D. (1824) from Marischal College, Aberdeen. He also published school textbooks on other subjects.

57 BUCHANAN, Colin. 1808

An Engraved system of bookkeeping ... Edinburgh: 1808.
(Not seen)
115p. 23.5cm.
REF: DM-51.
LOC: Watt Library, Greenock.

58 MORRISON, James. 1808

A Complete system of merchant's accounts containing the principles and modern improvements of bookkeeping in various sets of books by single and double entry. Edinburgh: James Ballantyne and co., 1808.

x,401p. 25cm.

REF: DM-43.

LOC: GP; E.

59 MORRISON, James. 1810

Elementary principles and rules of bookkeeping ... Glasgow: W. Lang, 1810.

34p. 17cm.

REF: -

LOC: GP.

60 SMITH, John. 1810

On a new ... plan. Tables for calculating interest at 5 per cent on any sum from £1 to £20,000 from 1 day to 365, and from 1 year to 10 years, accompanied by two short and simple tables for reducing to the rates of 3 and 4 per cent, with tables for calculating exchange and commission. Edinburgh: Mundell, Doig and Stevenson for Bell & Bradfute, 1810.

8,(6),392p. 21cm.

REF: -

LOC: NLS; BM.

61 FARQUHARSON, Alexander. 1813

The Rural accountant, or, A Practical system of farmers bookkeeping in three books viz. Waste book, journal and ledger together with all the subsidiary books thereto belonging ... Edinburgh: J. Orphoot for John and James Robertson, Booksellers, 1813.

112p. 22cm.

REF: -

LOC: NLS.

Farquharson was a teacher at the Commercial School, Kirkcaldy. His book is, he says, an attempt "to accommodate old principles to new subjects" and to dress up "the farmer in the habit of a merchant" (p.4).

62 MORRISON, James. 1813

The Young ladies' guide to practical arithmetic and bookkeeping ... Glasgow: 1813.

(Not seen)

REF: -

LOC: GP.

------2nd.ed. Glasgow: W. Lang, 1821.

viii,115p. 17cm.

LOC: GUL; NLS.

63 MORRISON, Charles. 1814

A Complete system of practical bookkeeping applicable to all types of business ... Glasgow: 1814.

(Not seen)

REF: DM-76.

LOC: -

-----3rd.ed. Glasgow: 1823.

xvi,304p. 22cm.

LOC: SE; GUL; GP; E; NLS; Columbia; Newcastle Univ. Lib.

-----4th.ed. Edinburgh: 1828.

xvi,312p. 22cm.

LOC: SE; GP; Aberdeen Public Library.

-----5th.ed. Edinburgh: 1834.

xvi,340p. 22cm.

LOC: SE; E; NLS.

-----6th.ed. Edinburgh: 1838.

LOC: SE; SG; E.

-----7th.ed. Glasgow: Richard Griffin & Co., 1843.

-----8th.ed. Glasgow: 1849.

Morrison was a teacher and practitioner in Glasgow.

64 MORRISON, James. 1814

A Compendium of practical arithmetic containing such rules only as are applicable to mercantile transactions ... 2nd.ed. Glasgow: 1814.

(Not seen)

REF: -

LOC: Hull Institute of Education.

-----3rd.ed. Glasgow: 1818.

LOC: BM.

-----4th.ed. Glasgow: 1822.

iv,175p. 18cm.

LOC: GP.

-----5th.ed. (stereo edition) Glasgow: 1824.

LOC: NLS.

-----(another edition) Glasgow: 1827.

LOC: GUL.

-----(another edition) Glasgow: 1829.

-----8th.ed. Glasgow: 1831.

LOC: GP.

-----10th.ed. Glasgow: 1837.

iv,200p. 17cm.

LOC: SE; GUL.

65 THOMSON, John. 1815

The Readiest reckoner in miniature containing accurate tables from one to ten thousand at the various prices from one farthing to one pound, also tables of interest ... Edinburgh: Oliver and Boyd, (1815).

160p. 11cm.

REF: -

LOC: NLS.

Robert Hamilton, LL.D., F.R.S.E.

(1743-1829)

(see item 40)

This portrait is reproduced here by permission of the Court of the University of Aberdeen.

James McClelland, C.A.
(Glasgow, 1799-1879)
(see item 106)

65 THOMSON, John. (cont.) 1815

The Readiest reckoner in miniature ...

-----(new edition) Edinburgh: (1883).
LOC: Oxford.

66 LESLIE, Sir John. 1817

The Philosophy of arithmetic ... Edinburgh: Abernethy and Walker for Archibald Constable, 1817.

iv,240p. 22cm.

REF: -
LOC: SE; GUL; GP; NLS; BM; Oxford; Cambridge.

-----2nd.ed. Edinburgh: 1820.

258p. 23cm.

LOC: SE; EUL; EP; NLS; BM.

Leslie was professor of mathematics in the University of Edinburgh. Arithmetic is "Deduced from its principles, and treated as a branch of liberal education". There is much historical illustration.

66.1 MORRISON, (Charles). 1819

Introduction to bookkeeping and business ... 2nd.ed. Glasgow: R. Chapman for Reid and Henderson, 1819.

xvi,272p. plates 22cm.

REF: -
LOC: SE.

67 BOAZ, James. 1820

Interval tables, interest tables, tables of the first day of each month in the nineteenth century ... Glasgow: Robert Chapman, 1820.

120p. 19cm.

REF: -
LOC: GUL; GP.

The GP copy has 132p., as an appendix of tables of interest at 5% is included.

The author describes himself as "Accountant, Glasgow".

68 MORRISON, Charles. 1820

The Young lady's guide to practical arithmetic ... to which is added the method of keeping accounts ... Glasgow: R. Chapman for Ogle, Allardice and Thomson, 1820.

xii,180p. 17cm.

REF: -
LOC: E; GUL; St. Andrews; NLS.

Illustrated by a "simple and concise set of books, applicable to the milliner, haberdasher and shopkeeper in general". Only pp. 121-168 deal with bookkeeping.

69 DUNN, Thomas. 1821

Tables of simple interest computed decimally ... Glasgow: Young, Gallie and co. for the author, 1821.

8+206p. 35cm.

REF: DM-334.
LOC: SE; NLS; BM

69 DUNN, Thomas. (cont.) 1821

Tables of simple interest ...

------(another edition) Glasgow: 1829.
LOC: GP.

Dunn was an accountant in Greenock.

70 MUNRO, Innes. 1821

A Guide to farm-bookkeeping ... Edinburgh: C. Stewart for John Anderson, 1821.

xxxii,139p. 26cm.

REF: -
LOC: SE; GUL; EUL; BM.

Munro was a practical farmer and had been a paymaster in the Army. There is a list of subscribers.

71 BOAZ, James and JAFFRAY, William. 1823

Interest tables at four per cent. Glasgow: for the authors, 1823.

viii,320p.

(Not seen)

REF: DM-118.
LOC: BM.

72 MARSHALL, James. 1823

Interest at four per cent.

(Not seen - in NLS special collection)

REF: DM-118.
LOC: NLS.

73 TROTTER, Alexander (of Dreghorn) 1825

A Method of farm bookkeeping exemplified by the forms and accounts actually practised by the author. Edinburgh: 1825.

(Not seen)

REF: -
LOC: EUL; BM.

74 HALLIDAY, J. 1826

The Complete ready reckoner containing accurate tables ... Dumfries: W. Carson, 1826.

200p. 12cm.

(Not seen, source: Trans. Dum. & Gall. N. H. & Antiq. Soc. v.18 (1931-32) pp.129-186)

REF: -
LOC: -

Dumfries County Libraries have a copy.

75 INGRAM, Alexander. 1826

The Principles of arithmetic explained and their application to real business clearly elucidated. Edinburgh: 1826.

(Not seen)

REF: DM-327.
LOC: BM.

75 INGRAM, Alexander. (cont.) 1826

The Principles of arithmetic ...

-----(another edition) Edinburgh: 1831.
108p. 15cm.
LOC: GUL.

-----4th.ed. Edinburgh: 1835.
LOC: St. Andrews; University Coll., London.

-----5th.ed. Edinburgh: 1841.
LOC: AUL; Maths Assoc., Leicester Univ.

-----30th.ed. Revised. Edinburgh: 1852.
LOC: BM.

-----42nd.ed. Remodelled and greatly enlarged by A. Trotter. Edinburgh: 1864.
LOC: NLS; BM.

-----50th.ed. Edinburgh: 1873.
LOC: BM.

-----52nd.ed. Edinburgh: 1875.
LOC: BM.

-----56th.ed. Edinburgh: 1881.
154p. 15cm.
LOC: NLS; BM.

-----57th.ed. Edinburgh: 1883.
LOC: NLS; BM.

-----58th.ed. Edinburgh: 1885.
LOC: NLS; BM.

-----60th.ed. Edinburgh: 1894.
LOC: NLS.

76 DAVIDSON, John and SCOTT, Robert. 1827

Arithmetic modernised, or, A Complete system of arithmetic adapted to modern practice ... the whole accommodated to the present state of trade ... Edinburgh: James Walker for Bell & Bradfute, 1827.
viii,233p. 18cm.
REF: -
LOC: EUL.

-----12th.ed. Improved and enlarged. Edinburgh: 1853.
xx,228+34p.
LOC: BM.

-----19th.ed. Edinburgh: 1869.
LOC: St. Andrews.

77 ACCOUNTANT, An. 1829

Principles of life annuities and assurances ... Edinburgh: Thomas Clark, 1829.
iv,114p. 22cm.
REF: -
LOC: SE.

78 MURRAY, Robert. 1830

A New system of commercial arithmetic, or, Guide to business and science for the use of schools ... Edinburgh: A. Balfour and co. for John Boyd, 1830.

vi,443p. 17cm.

REF: -

LOC: SE; GUL; BM; Maths Assoc., Leicester Univ.

The author describes himself as Master of the Commercial and Mathematical Academy, Edinburgh.

79 BRODIE, David. 1831

A Short set of bookkeeping by double entry ... Paisley: Neilson and Hay, 1831.

55p. 22cm.

REF: DM-50.

LOC: SE; GUL.

Described on the title page as "an Exercise for those who have made some progress in the Art", the set illustrates, with amusing incidents, the unsuccessful co-partnership of Simon Sober, George Greedy and Thomas Tippler. The appended list of subscribers includes a "canal treasurer" and three "accountants". Brodie was a teacher in Paisley.

80 DAVIDSON, John. 1834

The Young arithmetician's guide, being an easy introductory course of practical arithmetic for the use of schools. 2nd.ed. Edinburgh: James Walker for Bell & Bradfute, 1834.

125p. 15cm.

REF: -

LOC: GUL.

-----6th.ed. Edinburgh: 1841.

LOC: NLS.

81 STEWART, Robert C. 1834

A Treatise on arithmetic, in theory and practice ... Edinburgh: Stirling and Kenney, 1834.

x,228p. 15cm.

REF: -

LOC: SE.

-----(another edition) Edinburgh: 1864.

LOC: NLS.

The author is described on the title page as a teacher of writing, arithmetic and bookkeeping in Edinburgh.

82 JAMIESON, John. 1835

An Easy introduction to bookkeeping ... to which is added the system of farm bookkeeping ... Glasgow: David Robertson, 1835.

144p. 18cm.

REF: -

LOC: SE; E.

82 JAMIESON, John. (cont.) 1835

An Easy introduction to bookkeeping ...

"Expressly designed for schools" and including, with modifications, "the system of farm bookkeeping, for which the Highland Society of Scotland awarded their prize, in 1827; ... founded on the transactions of Alexander Trotter, esq., of Dreghorn" (see item 73 above).

83 (HUTTON, Charles). 1838

A Complete course of bookkeeping ... Dumfries: James Thorburn Creighton, 1838.

vi,96p. 19cm.

REF: YET-b.

LOC: SE.

84 HUTTON, Charles with additions by James TROTTER. 1838

A Complete treatise on bookkeeping. Edited by Alexander Ingram. A new edition with many important improvements and additions including new sets of books both by single and double entry, exemplifying the modern practice of bookkeeping by James Trotter. Edinburgh: Oliver and Boyd, 1838.

252p. 18cm.

Note: all copies located consist of pp,141-252 only, i.e. the additions of James Trotter.

REF: DM-326; YET-b.

LOC: SE; GUL; E.

-----(another edition) Edinburgh and London: 1840.

LOC: E; BM.

-----(another edition) Edinburgh: 1853.

LOC: BM.

-----A new edition. Edinburgh and London: 1856.

LOC: E; Newcastle Univ. Lib.

-----(another edition) Edinburgh and London: 1858.

LOC: E; NLS.

-----(another edition) Edinburgh and London: 1863.

LOC: E.

-----(another edition) Edinburgh and London: (1870).

LOC: E.

-----(another edition) Edinburgh: (1886).

85 TAYLOR, Donald. 1838

The Counting house manual, or, The Principles and practice of double entry bookkeeping ... Glasgow: David Robertson, 1838.

vii,252p. 17cm.

REF: DM-339/40.

LOC: GUL.

85.1 DEFOE, Daniel. 1839

The Complete English tradesman ... with notes. Edinburgh: William and Robert Chambers, 1839.

86p. 26cm.

REF: -

LOC: Harvard; Boston Public Library.

This appears to be the only edition published in Scotland. The first edition was published in London in 1726.

Despite Defoe's greater fame as the author of "Robinson Crusoe" (written when he was 59), he devoted most of his life to writing on commercial and economic subjects. Chapter XX in his "Complete English Tradesman" is concerned with bookkeeping. The tradesman is enjoined to keep books of account as an essential aid to prosperity. Defoe complains that, even amongst those tradesmen who do keep books, some cease to do so because they are afraid to find out how badly their business is doing, whereas in case of bankruptcy, creditors view with more favour the bankrupt who has kept his books up-to-date. (Defoe had personal experience of this.) A tradesman without his books is "like a married woman withour her certificate".

Finally, he exhorts: "Next to being prepared for death, with respect to Heaven and his soul, a tradesman should always be in a state of preparation for death, in respect of his books ..."

85.2 THE PLEASING Art of Money-Catching 1840

The Pleasing Art of Money-Catching and the Way to Thrive by Turning a Penny to advantage; with a New Method of Regulating Daily Expenses. Falkirk, 1840.

24p. 16cm.

(Not seen)

REF: -

LOC: -

86 WATERSTON, William. 1840

A Manual of commerce, being a compendium of reckoning tables ... exchange tables, simple interest tables, compound interest, annuities and life assurance...Edinburgh: Oliver and Boyd, 1840.

(Not seen)

REF: -

LOC: BM.

------2nd.ed. Edinburgh: 1844.

LOC: BM.

------New edition, greatly enlarged. Edinburgh: 1859.

LOC: BM.

------New edition, revised. Edinburgh: 1860.

vii,300p. 17cm.

LOC: NLS; BM.

------New edition, revised. Edinburgh: 1862.

304p. 17cm.

LOC: NLS; BM.

------New edition, revised. Edinburgh: 1865.

LOC: NLS; BM.

James Meston, C.A.
(Aberdeen, 1821-1892)
(see item 113)

Sir John Mann, C.A.
(Glasgow, 1864-1955)
(see item 297)

86 WATERSTON, William. (cont.) 1840

A Manual of commerce ...

-----New edition, revised. Edinburgh: (1871).
LOC: BM.

-----New edition, revised. Edinburgh: 1875.
LOC: BM.

-----New edition, revised. Edinburgh: 1884.
LOC: BM.

-----New edition, revised. Edinburgh: 1889.
LOC: BM.

87 MILLAR, Thomas H. 1841

A Practical introduction to life and fire assurance ... Edinburgh: Ballantyne and Hughes for the author and Oliver and Boyd, 1841.

(4),144p. 23cm.

REF: -
LOC: GUL; BM.

The author describes himself as "Accountant, Edinburgh".

88 HOWATT, John. 1842

A Compendium of practical bookkeeping ... Glasgow: 1842.

(Not seen - source: B.F. Foster: "Double entry elucidated", 5th.ed. London, 1852,p.x. and H.J. Eldridge: "The Evolution of the science of bookkeeping", London, 1931, p.56.)

89 "CALCULATOR" 1843

Counting house manual and introduction to business, being an outline of practical bookkeeping. Merchants, manufacturers and wholesale and retail dealers are instructed in the correct principles of ascertaining a true state of their affairs and exact income from trade at all times; also simple rules for calculating interest and discounts for any given time at any given rate per cent ... Edinburgh: Oliver and Boyd, 1843.

64p. 24cm.

REF: -
LOC: E; NLS; BM.

Claimed by its author as being "of extreme simplicity and general utility".

89.1 STEPHENS, Henry. 1844

The Book of the farm. 3 vols. Edinburgh: William Blackwood & Sons, 1844.

vol. I xix,670p. plates. 24.5cm.
vol. II (4),728p. plates. 24.5cm.
vol. III vi,678p. plates. 24.5cm.

REF: -
LOC: NLS; BM.

-----2nd.ed. 2 vols. Edinburgh, 1851/2.
LOC: NLS; BM.

-----3rd.ed. 2 vols. Edinburgh, 1871.
LOC: BM.

89.1 STEPHENS, Henry. (cont.) 1844
The Book of the farm ...

-----4th.ed. 3 vols. revised by James Macdonald. Edinburgh: 1891.
LOC: SE; BM.

-----5th.ed. 3 vols. Edinburgh, 1908.
LOC: BM.

The work contains a chapter on bookkeeping, which was also published as a separate booklet (see item 94.1). The main work contains superb engraved illustrations of farm animals.

89.2 MERCHANT's and banker's commercial pocket guide: c.1845
A manual of banking and commerce. New ed. Glasgow: W.R. McPhun, n.d., c.1845.
129p. 12cm.
REF: -
LOC:

90 WALLACE, Robert. 1847
The Pocket guide to commercial bookkeeping. A practical treatise of merchant accounts by single and double entry ... 11th.thousand. Glasgow: W.R. M'Phun, and Edinburgh: Oliver and Boyd, 1847.
156p. 12cm.
REF: -
LOC: GUL; E; BM.

-----(another edition) Glasgow: 1856.
LOC: E.

Reprinted in "thousands".

The author is described on the title page as Professor Wallace. He claims that his method of keeping the Day Book is "a modification or rather an improvement of the principle of check of double columns invented by Mr. Jones" (pp.10-11).

91 INGLIS, William. 1849
Bookkeeping by single and double entry with an appendix containing explanations of mercantile terms and transactions, questions in bookkeeping ... Edinburgh and London: W. & R. Chambers, 1849.
188,xxi p. 20cm.
REF: -
LOC: NLS.

-----(another edition) Edinburgh: 1858.
LOC: BM.

-----New edition. Edinburgh: (1861).
LOC: E; BM.

-----New edition. Edinburgh: 1866.
LOC: BM.

-----New edition. Edinburgh: 1867.
LOC: BM.

91 INGLIS, William. (cont.) 1849
Bookkeeping by single and double entry ...

------(another edition) Edinburgh: 1881.
184,xxiii. 18.5cm.
LOC: SE.

91.1 INSTITUTE OF ACCOUNTANTS OF GLASGOW 1853
Deed of constitution and rules or regulations. Glasgow (?), 1853.
14p. 21cm.
REF: -
LOC: SE.

92 MacLAREN, James. 1853
An Improved system of practical book keeping according to single entry ... 6th.ed. Edinburgh: 1853.
(Not seen)
REF: -
LOC: BM.

------11th.ed. Edinburgh: (n.d.)
(Not seen, ref. E.Stevelinck, Acc.Mag.v.76(1972)p.393-398.)
LOC: GUL.

93 MacLAREN, James. 1853
Set of books adapted to MacLaren's book keeping ... Edinburgh: (1853).
(Not seen)
REF: -
LOC: BM.

94 STEWART, Robert. 1853
A Practical treatise on arithmetic, arranged for pupils in classes ... New edition, improved ... Edinburgh: 1853.
(Not seen)
REF: -
LOC: BM.

94.1 STEPHENS, Henry. 1856
A Practical system of farm bookkeeping. Edinburgh: William Blackwood & Sons, 1856.
(Not seen)
REF: -
LOC: BM.

------6th.ed. Edinburgh, 1886.
(2),16,(2) p. 24cm.
LOC: SE; BM.
See item 89.1.

95 MacLEAN, John Dalziel. 1857
Bookkeeping for the classroom and counting-house by double and single entry with an appendix of commercial forms. 7th.ed. Glasgow and London: W. Collins, sons and co., (1857).
xiii,213p. 18cm.
(Collins school series)
REF: -
LOC: E.

95 MacLEAN, John Dalziel. (cont.) 1857

Bookkeeping for the classroom and counting-house ...

The author appears to have been a teacher at Edinburgh Academy and later the High School of Glasgow.

96 MONTGOMERIE, Archibald. 1858

Bookkeeping for every business: a manual of the principles of bookkeeping by single and double entry. Adapted for use in schools or self-instruction in the counting house. New edition. Glasgow: George Watson, 1858.

96p. 19cm.

REF: -

LOC: GUL; BM.

The author was Rector of Greenock Academy.

97 BRYCE, J. 1860

Treatise on bookkeeping by double and single entry. A new edition, greatly enlarged. Edinburgh: Adam and Charles Black, 1860.

viii,217p. 2 plates. 20cm.

REF: -

LOC: SE; NLS; BM.

98 MORRISON, C. 1860

A Series of improved mercantile forms and accounts, commercial correspondence, etc. Glasgow: W.R. McPhun, (1860).

(Not seen)

REF: -

LOC: BM.

99 CARTER, F. Hayne. 1861

Practical bookkeeping adapted to commercial and judicial accounting ... Edinburgh: Edmonston and Douglas, 1861.

155p. 23cm.

REF: -

LOC: NLS; BM.

-----2nd.ed. Edinburgh: 1874.

x,240p. 23cm.

LOC: SE; EUL; E; NLS; BM.

-----3rd.ed. Edinburgh: 1875.

LOC: E; BM.

-----4th.ed. Edinburgh: 1878.

LOC: SE; EUL; E; BM.

-----5th.ed. Edinburgh: 1885.

LOC: NLS; BM.

-----6th.ed. Revised and corrected by Fred. W. Carter. Edinburgh: 1890.

x,264p. 11 hinged plates. 23cm.

LOC: SE; EUL; GUL; E; NLS; BM.

In the introduction refers to Mair's Bookkeeping Modernised (item 37 above) as "a work elaborate, and now almost unintelligible"; concludes with the advice that "Reticence is one of the most valuable gifts of a Book-keeper; for however excellent his other qualifications may be, let him but indulge in chattering propensities, and he is worse than useless". The chapters in between cover a miscellany of topics e.g.

99 CARTER, F. Hayne. (cont.) 1861
Practical bookkeeping ...

life assurance companies' and shipping companies' books, solicitors' accounts, judicial factory and curatory accounts, books for charitable or public institutions.

100 FAIRBAIRN, James. 1861
Fairbairn's interest tables nos. 1 and 2 for facilitating the calculation of interest on current accounts. Edinburgh: 1861.
(Not seen)
REF: -
LOC: BM.

101 IRELAND: Commissioners of National Education. 1863
Elements of bookkeeping in a series of short examples for the use of schools. Edinburgh: William P. Nimmo, 1863.
126p. 17cm.
REF: -
LOC: SE.

102 TURNBULL, Andrew Hugh. 1863
Tables of compound interest and annuities ... Edinburgh: Adam and Charles Black, 1863.
xxvii,143p. 22cm.
REF: -
LOC: SE; BM.

102.1 ELEMENTS OF book-keeping 1864
Elements of book-keeping in a series of short examples. For the use of schools. Glasgow: William Collins, 1864.
126p. 17cm.
REF: -
LOC: E.

102.2 ESSON, G. Auldjo. 1866
Notes on Scotch bankruptcy law and practice ... Edinburgh: Edmonston and Douglas, 1866.
xi,90p. 23cm.
REF: -
LOC: SE.

Chapter XII is on the supervision and control of the accountant in bankruptcy.

103 INGLIS, William. 1866
Farm bookkeeping. Edinburgh and London: W. & R. Chambers, 1866.
40p. 19cm.
REF: -
LOC: NLS; BM.

104 INGLIS, William. 1866

Single entry bookkeeping. New edition. Edinburgh: W. & R. Chambers, 1866.

(Not seen)

REF: -

LOC: BM.

------(another edition) Edinburgh: 1894.

An abridged version of Bookkeeping by single and double entry (item 91 above) "for the convenience of those who may not require a knowledge of the entire system" (from the introduction to item 91).

105 BELL, John. 1867

Examination questions in bookkeeping by double entry, with answers. Edinburgh and London: W. & R. Chambers, 1867.

95p. 20cm.

(Chambers' educational course)

REF: -

LOC: NLS; BM.

105.1 CHARTERED ACCOUNTANTS OF SCOTLAND post-1867

Royal Charter - and bye-laws, rules and regulations. Glasgow: J.C. Erskine & Sons (?), for The Society of Accountants in Aberdeen, n.d. (post-1867).

8+19p. 21cm.

REF: -

LOC: SE.

105.2 BROWN, Robert E. 1869

The Book of the landed estate containing directions for the management and development of the resources of landed property. Edinburgh: William Blackwood & Sons, 1869.

xiv,505p. 23.5cm.

REF: -

LOC: SE; BM.

Contains a chapter on estate bookkeeping.

106 McCLELLAND, J. 1869

The Origin and present organisation of the profession of chartered accountancy in Scotland. Glasgow: 1869.

24p. 22cm.

REF: -

LOC: SG; NLS; L; SE (photocopy).

McClelland was the first President of The Institute of Accountants and Actuaries in Glasgow, 1853-1864. He emphasizes the differences in Scottish and English bankruptcy law and practice and their effect on the accountancy profession. (See item 315).

107 NELSON, James. 1871

Bookkeeping by double entry exemplified in a simple set of books principally for retailers ... Edinburgh and Glasgow: W. Blackwood and sons for J. Menzies, 1871.

xvi,61p. 22cm.

107 NELSON, James. (cont.) 1871

Bookkeeping by double entry ...

REF: -

LOC: SE; GUL; BM.

Emphasizes the need for retailers to use double entry instead of, as so often suggested, single entry.

108 EDINBURGH: General Board of Lunacy. 1883

Rules and forms ... regulating the keeping of the accounts of district boards of lunacy ... Edinburgh: for the General Board of Lunacy, (1883).

25p. 32cm.

REF: -

LOC: SE.

109 MacCALL, John Campbell. 1884

The Art and practice of account keeping. Reprint from Transactions of the Insurance and Actuarial Society of Glasgow, 1884.

12p. 21cm.

REF: -

LOC: SE; BM.

110 ALLEN, George. 1885

Allen's forty lessons in practical double entry bookkeeping arranged as a text book for use in Graded and High Schools as a book of reference for business men. Edinburgh: James Gemmell, 1885.

viii,96p. 24cm.

Published North Carolina: Richardson, 1885. (National Union Catalogue)

REF: -

LOC: NLS; BM.

An American school text book, which went to five editions in the USA: see H.C. Bentley and R.S. Leonard, Bibliography of Works on Accounting by American Authors (1934), 2v. v.1 p.72-3.

111 McKIE, David. 1885

Monthly interest tables at 1,1½ and 2 per cent. Edinburgh: George Waterston and sons, (1885).

16p. 26cm.

REF: -

LOC: NLS.

112 TOLMIE, David. 1885

An Elementary treatise on bookkeeping by double entry for the use of schools and for self-tuition, to which are appended rules for rapid and concise methods of calculation. Glasgow: Blackie and son, 1885.

63p. 19cm.

(Blackie's elementary text books)

REF: -

LOC: NLS; BM.

Tolmie was a teacher of bookkeeping in London. He points out in the preface that "by the provisions of the New (English) Bankruptcy Act, it is now a statutory offence, punishable by imprisonment, for those in business on their own account, to neglect to keep a correct set of books".

113 MESTON, James. 1886

Opening address (to) the Aberdeen Accountants' Students' Society. Aberdeen: Cornwall and son, 1886.

14p. 19cm.

REF: -

LOC: SE.

James Meston, (1821-1892) was one of the founders, in 1867, of The Society of Accountants in Aberdeen. (See item 319).

114 CHARTERED ACCOUNTANTS' STUDENTS' SOCIETY OF EDINBURGH. 1886

Transactions. V.1 (1886-88) - v.25(1913-14)

Annual or biennial publication.

115 HINES, G., JONES, B. and PUMPHREY, H. 1887

Easy bookkeeping for small co-operative societies ... by authority of the Southern section of Central Co-operative Board. Edinburgh: Edinburgh co-operative printing co., ltd., 1887.

24p. 21cm.

REF: -

LOC: E; BM.

115.1 HOWARD, C. Frusher. 1888

Howard's Anglo-American Art of reckoning. Edinburgh: John Menzies & Co., 1888.

143p. 17cm.

REF: -

LOC: SE; NLS.

According to the Preface, phenomenal sales of this book were achieved (370,000 by this edition). The author, an American, was an indefatigable promoter of his own work and, in pursuit of more sales, set up his pitch at the International Exhibition at Glasgow in 1888 (hence this Scottish edition). Reviews quoted at the end of the book give the impression that he charmed his audiences.

116 LISLE, George. 1888

Deposit receipt interest tables. Edinburgh: George Waterston and sons, 1888.

47p. 24cm.

REF: -

LOC: SE.

The first of a number of books by a leading text book writer and lecturer at Heriot-Watt College, Edinburgh.

117 BELL, John. 1889

Chambers's examination bookkeeping with civil service and other papers fully solved. Edinburgh and London: W. & R. Chambers, 1889.

142p. 20cm.

REF: -

LOC: NLS; BM.

------(another edition) Edinburgh and London: 1908.

LOC: E; NLS.

117 BELL, John. (cont.) 1889

Chambers's examination bookkeeping ...

Author is described on the title page as LL.D., M.A. and as Examiner in Book-keeping to the College of Preceptors, London. A special paper on Government Departmental Book-keeping, compiled by R.U. Morgan of the War Office, is included.

118 MILLAR, Robert Cockburn. 1889

The Accountant's handbook of interest states, decimal calculations, consignments and joint accounts, etc. Edinburgh: Neill and co. for John Menzies, 1889.

viii,105p. 22cm.

REF: -

LOC: SE; E; NLS; BM.

-----Third edition in two parts. Edinburgh: 1891.

LOC: BM.

Millar was a lecturer at the Heriot-Watt College, Edinburgh, and later (1910-1913) President of The Society of Accountants in Edinburgh.

119 M'CLYMONT, John W. 1890

Lawyers' cash bookkeeping, being an abbreviated system founded on the divisionally arranged cash book. Glasgow: William Hodge and co., 1890.

30p. (2 fold.) 19cm.

REF: -

LOC: E; NLS; BM.

A purely cash system with credit transactions excluded. The author was a solicitor in Ayr.

120 LASSEN, Claudius. 1891

The Commercial guide: systematic book keeping by single and double entry ... supplemented by the book keeping system taught in Heriot-Watt College, Edinburgh. Edinburgh and Glasgow: T. & A. Constable for John Menzies and co., 1891.

xii,262p. 24cm.

REF: -

LOC: GUL; E; BM.

Interesting only for the indications it gives of the book-keeping methods taught at Heriot-Watt College.

121 LISLE, George. 1891

Local Government (Scotland) Act, 1889, on the bookkeeping and forms of accounts required by the County Councils under the ... Act ... with forms of cash books, ledgers, journals and specimens of accounts with explanations and instructions. Edinburgh: George Stewart and co., (1891).

81p. 25cm.

REF: -

LOC: E; NLS.

122 MacLAUCHLAN, James John. 1891
On life assurance bookkeeping - on some formulas for use in life office valuations ... Reprinted from Transactions of the Actuarial Society of Edinburgh, v.2, 1891.
(Not seen)
REF: -
LOC: BM; E.

123 CHAMBERS, William and Robert. (Publishers) 1892
Chambers' bookkeeping. Revised and adapted from Inglis's bookkeeping ... 3 parts. Edinburgh and London: W. & R. Chambers, 1892-96.
3v. 199p. 18cm.
REF: -
LOC: NLS; BM.

124 MacLEAN, John Dalziel. 1892
Bookkeeping as a specific subject in stages I, II and III, with numerous exercises to suit the requirements of the graduated course approved by the education department. Glasgow: J.N. MacKinley, 1892.
3v. (40; 72; ?)p. 18cm.
REF: -
LOC: NLS (parts I and II only.)

125 MacLEAN, John Dalziel. 1892
An Introduction to countinghouse and examination bookkeeping with examination papers ... and an appendix on government bookkeeping. Glasgow: J.N. MacKinley, 1892.
viii,139p. 19cm.
REF: -
LOC: SE; NLS: BM.

The author of items 124 and 125 was a teacher at the High School of Glasgow. (See also item 95.)

125.1 STRATHIE, David. 1892
Fixed machinery. A paper delivered to members of the Glasgow Institute of Accountants' Debating Society, on 15th December, 1892.
18p. 21cm.
REF: -
LOC: E.

126 HARDIE, William. 1893
Manual of bookkeeping for law agents with forms of trust accounts. Edinburgh: William Green and sons, 1893.
(6),55p. 25cm.
REF: -
LOC: SE; GP; E; NLS; BM.

127 HARDIE, William and ALLAN, Alexander. 1893
Manual of bookkeeping by double entry. 2nd.ed. Edinburgh: William Green and sons, 1893.
41p. 22cm.
REF: -
LOC: E; NLS; BM.

127 HARDIE, William and ALLAN, Alexander. (cont.) 1893
Manual of bookkeeping by double entry.

Written mainly for wholesalers and retailers. The authors were C.A.s in Edinburgh and Glasgow respectively.

128 COLQUHOUN, Dr. James. 1894
Corporation finance. A lecture delivered to the Glasgow Institute of Accountants' Debating Society. Published privately, 1894.
17p. 21cm.
REF: -
LOC: SG; GP.

The corporation referred to is Glasgow. The author was Convener of the Finance Committee of the Glasgow Police Commission.

129 LISLE, George. 1894
Elementary bookkeeping. Edinburgh and London: W. & R. Chambers, 1894.
168p. 20cm.
REF: -
LOC: NLS; BM.

130 LISLE, George. 1894
Examination papers of the Chartered Accountants of Scotland General Examining Board, set Dec., 1893. With answers by George Lisle. Edinburgh: W. Green and sons, 1894.
viii,84p.
(Not seen)
REF: -
LOC: BM.

131 NORTON, George Pepler. 1894
Balancing for expert bookkeepers. Edinburgh and Glasgow: John Menzies and co., 1894.
xii,61p. 24cm.
REF: -
LOC: E; BM.

Norton was an English Chartered Accountant and the author also of Textile Manufacturers' Book-keeping, (Huddersfield, 1889).

132 ROSS, John Munn. 1894
The Law relating to audits and auditors. A lecture delivered to the Chartered Accountants' Debating Society of Glasgow. Published privately, 1894.
16p. 21cm.
REF: -
LOC: SG.

A review of the cases with suggestions for reform.

133 STUART, Alexander Moody. 1894
Bookkeeping: observations and suggestions. Edinburgh: 1894.
(Not seen - reference Accountants' Index, 1920.)
REF: -
LOC: -

134 TODD, James. 1894

Government examination papers for leaving certificates, elementary day schools and evening continuation schools. Stirling: 1894.

23p. 16cm.

(Not seen - not available at the time of visit to library).

REF: -
LOC: E.

135 BOGAL, John Douglas Stewart and ATTFIELD, J.H. 1895

M'Dougall's bookkeeping for elementary schools ... Edinburgh and London: McDougalls, 1895-6.

(Not seen - reference <u>Accountants' Index</u>, 1920).

REF: -
LOC: -

136 MARTIN, James. 1895

The Accountant profession: a public danger. Glasgow: 1895.

29p. 22cm.

REF: -
LOC: SG; NLS; SE (photocopy).

-----2nd.ed. Glasgow: 1896.
LOC: BM.

A polemic against the "preposterous pretensions of the chartered accountants and their mock heroic treatment of other accountants" (p.2). <u>See also</u> items 139,142,143 and 169 below.

137 ROBERTSON, J.A. 1895

The Business of an accountant. An address to members of the Glasgow Institute of Accountants' Debating Society. Published privately, 1895.

20p. 21cm.

REF: -
LOC: SG.

Discusses bank audits, investigations, apportionment of capital and income, and the accounts of investment companies.

137.1 SCOTTISH ACCOUNTANT, THE. 1895

The organ of the Scottish Institute of Accountants. vol. 1. (no record found of further vols.) Glasgow: 1895.

4to.

(Not seen; temporarily not available)

REF:
LOC: NLS.

This body, a small mainly provincial group formed in 1881, attempted, unsuccessfully, to rival the Edinburgh, Glasgow and Aberdeen C.A. bodies.

138 BROWN, Nicol. 1896

Specimens of working records and account books designed for gold mining companies. Glasgow: Duncan Campbell and son, 1896.

viii,30 11. 40cm.

(The specimens are bound between the leaves.)

REF: -
LOC: SE.

A set of model forms.

139 MARTIN, James. 1896

The Accountant 'CA' case. The Society of Accountants in Edinburgh and others against the Corporation of Accountants, Ltd. and others. Was there a misapplication of the law? Glasgow: William Hodge and co., 1896.

46p. 22cm.

REF: -

LOC: SE.

The Court of Session held in 1893 that the three Scottish chartered bodies were entitled to have James Martin and James L. Addie and the five other original members of "The Corporation of Accountants, Limited" interdicted from using for professional purposes, or as a professional designation, the letters C.A., or any other letters or words calculated to lead the public to believe that they were members of one or other of the bodies of accountants in Scotland, which were incorporated by royal charter: Society of Accountants in Edinburgh and Others v. Corporation of Accountants, Limited and Others, 20 R.750.

This is one of a number of pamphlets in which Martin uninhibitedly gives his own views of the case. See also items 142,143 and 169 below.

Martin, later Sir James Martin, was one of the founders of the Society of Incorporated Accountants and Auditors in 1885 and was president of the Society 1922-23 and 1935. For an obituary see The Accountant, v.93, (1935) p.292.

140 BLACKWOOD (William) AND SONS. (Publishers). 1897

The Accountant's Magazine. v.1 (1897) -

Monthly except August and September.

Intended as "a practical business journal for practical business men" and from the first closely associated with the Scottish chartered societies. The main articles in v.1 dealt with: causes and effects of the fall in the rate of interest; trust-deeds for creditors; parish council accounts and their audit; eminent accountants of the past; depreciation; the law relating to money securities; fee and liferent; the audit of life assurance company books; the Sale of Goods Act, 1893; the comparative costs of winding up bankrupt estates in Scotland and in England; the audit of the accounts of the police burghs; unclaimed bank deposits; the metric system of weights and measures; building societies; the bibliography of bookkeeping (by Richard Brown); recent currency proposals; depreciation of ships in relation to assessment for income tax; limited liability company reform.

From 1951 the magazine has been published monthly by The Institute of Chartered Accountants of Scotland.

141 BROWN, Nicol. 1897

The Organisation of gold-mining business, with specimens of the departmental report books and account books. Glasgow: Duncan Campbell and son, 1897.

v,177p. 33cm.

141 BROWN, Nicol. (cont.) 1897

The Organisation of gold-mining business ...

REF: -

LOC: SE; NLS; BM.

In effect an extended version of Brown's other book, item 138 above.

142 MARTIN, James. 1897

Did the devil win the toss? or, The Lie triumphant in the law courts, an exposure. Glasgow: Carter and Pratt, 1897.

32p. 22cm.

REF: -

LOC: SE.

The chapter headings are: the lie, the plot, the shuffle, the design, the excuse, the float, the conclusion. <u>See</u> item 139 above.

143 MARTIN, James. 1897

The Sanctification of the lie. Grace, grace unto it! A tribute to the Queen's sixty years' reign. Glasgow: Carter and Pratt, 1897.

39p. 22cm.

REF: -

LOC: SE.

Includes an Open Letter to the Secretary for Scotland, and the comment that chartered accountants put the initials C.A. "upon their intimations of births, their marriages and deaths, nay, even on their tombstones" (p.33-34). <u>See</u> item 139 above.

144 HENDERSON, Richard. 1898

Accounting.

(<u>in</u> - The Young estate manager's guide. Edinburgh: William Blackwood and sons, 1898. 19cm. p.241-259. (Ch.15)).

REF: -

LOC: SE; NLS; BM.

According to the author accounting is "not a very difficult branch of estate management" calling "more for close attention to daily routine than for the display of skill in dealing with sums" (p.241).

145 TURNBULL, Andrew D. Lindsay. 1898

Some suggestions in regard to life office accounting, including, <u>inter alia</u>, an arrangement of the American card system suitable for the requirements of British offices. Reprint from <u>Transactions of the Actuarial Society of Edinburgh</u>, v.4. Edinburgh: T. & A. Constable for C. & E. Layton, London, 1898.

65p. 23cm.

REF: -

LOC: E.

The author was Assistant Secretary of the Caledonian Insurance Company. He comments on pp.159-160 (of the <u>Transactions</u>)

145 TURNBULL, Andrew D. Lindsay. (cont.) 1898

Some suggestions in regard to life office accounting ... that 'The words "To" before debits and "By" before credits should never be written. They are a mere waste of space and a waste of time. Even a book-keeper, who is inclined to forget which is the debit and which is the credit side of an account, is not kept correct by the use of these cabalistic words.'

146 BARNETSON, James. 1899

McDougall's exercises in bookkeeping. Edinburgh: McDougall's educational co., (1899).

2v. (32; 32)p. 18cm.

REF: -

LOC: NLS; BM.

147 LISLE, George. 1899

Accounting in theory and practice ... Edinburgh: W. Green and sons, 1899. Reprinted New York: Arno Press, 1976.

xiv,426p. 23cm.

REF: -

LOC: NLS; BM.

-----(another edition) Edinburgh: 1906.

LOC: EUL; GP.

-----A new edition. Edinburgh: 1909.

LOC: SE; NLS; BM.

A text book of "advanced book-keeping and accounting" (preface). The topics covered include branch accounts, departmental accounts, "the card or loose-sheet system of keeping ledger accounts", reserves and reserve funds, sinking funds, goodwill, depreciation, apportionment, trust and executry accounts, partnership, joint stock companies, manufacturers' accounts, cost accounts, foreign currencies and branches, income tax, hire purchase system of acquiring railway wagons, investigations, auditing.

148 SOMERVILLE, J. 1899

Bookkeeping (by double entry) made easy, or, How to balance, quickly and correctly, any number of ledgers (presented in a nutshell). Leith: MacKenzie and Storrie, (1899).

8+8p. 21cm.

REF: -

LOC: NLS; BM.

149 FINDLATER, John. 1900

Bookkeeping by double entry explained. 3rd.ed. Edinburgh: Oliver and Boyd, 1900.

72p. 18cm.

First published London, 1868.

REF: -

LOC: E; BM.

Refers to, but does not elaborate upon, explanation of debit and credit by increases and decreases; recommends use of a Balance Account in the ledger. The author describes himself as "Accountant, Glasgow".

150 M'KIE, David. 1900

Bank bookkeeping. Edinburgh: Blackwood and son, 1900.
97p. 22cm.

REF: -
LOC: E; BM.

-----(2nd.ed.) Edinburgh: 1903.
104p. 23cm.
LOC: SE; NLS; E; BM.

-----3rd.ed. Edinburgh: 1907.
LOC: E; BM.

-----4th.ed. revised by F.H. Allan. Edinburgh: 1918.
LOC: E; NLS; BM.

Based upon a series of lectures published in The Accountants' Magazine (see item 140). M'Kie was at one time Chief Accountant of the National Bank of Scotland; Allan was editor of The Scottish Bankers' Magazine. The preface to the 4th.ed. refers to the "widespread adoption of the Burrough's Adding Machine".

151 SCOTT, Robert. 1901

New century bookkeeping for business people. Glasgow: N. Adshead and sons for W. & R. Holmes, 1901.
112p. 19cm.

REF: -
LOC: GP; E; NLS; BM.

Illustrates the business of a manufacturer who is also a flour merchant, but there is only a very slight treatment of cost accounting.

152 LISLE, George. (editor) 1903

Encyclopaedia of accounting. Edinburgh: William Green and sons, 1903-1907.
8v. (531; 517; 508; 508; 508; 496; 496; 512)p. 26cm.

REF: -
LOC: SE; SG; EUL; GP; E; NLS; BM; L.

These eight volumes (two of them containing forms and precedents) and 4,076 pages represent the most ambitious accountancy publishing project ever attempted in Scotland. The contributors include Lisle himself, William Annan, Arthur L. Bowley (the economist and statistician), Richard Brown, Lawrence R. Dicksee (professor of accounting in the University of Birmingham and author of several standard texts), Th. Limperg jr. of the Netherlands, John Mann jr., James Martin (see item 139), R.C. Millar (see item 118), Francis W. Pixley (author of the first British text on auditing) and Arthur F. Whinney.

There is some emphasis on accounting for different types of enterprise, e.g. building societies, collieries, pawnbrokers, printers, railways, tramways, wine merchants. Of more interest to the accounting historian are the articles on: accounting in its relation to economics (Victor V. Branford), auditing (Dicksee), balance sheets (Lisle: he traces the "traditional" British balance sheet form to the Companies Act, 1862), cost records or

152 LISLE, George. (editor) (cont.) 1903

Encyclopaedia of accounting.

factory accounting (Mann), depreciation (Edwin Guthrie), factory organization and costing arrangements (Cossar Mackenzie), goodwill (Sidney S. Dawson), oncost or expenses (Mann: see also item 290) and reserves and reserve funds (Dawson: secret reserves, he writes, "cannot be recommended, for it is quite as incorrect in principle to understate a company's position as it is to overstate it").

153 LITTLE, Robert. 1903

The Principles of double entry bookkeeping explained and illustrated. Edinburgh: R. Grant and son, 1903.

49p. 22cm.

REF: -

LOC: E; BM.

154 McKIE, David. 1903

Tables of compound interest and annuities ... Edinburgh: Andrew Baxendine, 1903.

120p. 27cm.

REF: -

LOC: EUL; NLS; BM.

-----New edition. Edinburgh: 1911.

LOC: BM.

154.1 MACLEOD, John M. 1903

Exhibition accounts and finance and the system of checking income and expenditure. Being a paper read to the Glasgow Accountants' Students' Society on 27th November, 1902. For private circulation. Glasgow: James Maclehose, 1903.

12,13p. Typescript. 33cm.

REF: -

LOC: E.

155 SCOTT, Robert. 1903

Graphic bookkeeping exercises. Glasgow and London: Wm. Collins, sons and co., (1903).

55p.

REF: -

LOC: NLS; BM.

155.1 CHARTERED ACCOUNTANTS OF SCOTLAND. 1904

Charter of incorporation, bye-laws, rules and regulations. Glasgow: James C. Erskine & Sons for The Institute of Accountants and Actuaries in Glasgow, 1904.

35p. 24cm.

REF: -

LOC: SE.

-----(another edition) Glasgow: 1911.

38p. 24cm.

LOC: SE.

155.2 CHARTERED ACCOUNTANTS OF SCOTLAND. 1904

Charter of incorporation, rules, regulations and bye-laws. Edinburgh: T. & A. Constable for The Society of Accountants in Edinburgh, 1904.

32p. 21cm.

REF: -

LOC: SE.

156 DODD, Arthur Francis. 1904

Railway accounts and their audit. (Edinburgh: 1904).

46p. 25cm.

(Not seen - reference ICAEW catalogue, 1937, but can no longer be located in that library.)

REF: -

LOC: -

157 GLASGOW CHARTERED ACCOUNTANTS' STUDENTS' SOCIETY. 1904

Transactions. v.1(1902-1904) - v.12(1914-1915).

Annual or biennial publication.

158 WARDHAUGH, John Broadfoot. 1904

The Accountant's digest ... Edinburgh: William Green and sons, 1904.

xv,210p. 22cm.

REF: -

LOC: SE; E; NLS; BM.

------2nd.ed. revised and enlarged. Edinburgh: 1912.

xxxv,366p. 22cm.

LOC: SE; GP; BM.

Aim of the book is to "furnish a concise and systematically arranged statement of the law relating to four important branches of the business of an Accountant", viz: bankruptcy proceedings; public companies; audit of county council, parish council and town council accounts; judicial factories.

Subsequently the work was published in four separate parts.

159 BROWN, Richard. 1905

A History of accounting and accountants, edited and partly written by Richard Brown. Edinburgh: T.C. & E.C. Jack, 1905.

xvi,459p. 26cm.

REF: -

LOC: SE; SG; EUL; GUL; EP; GP; NLS; BM; L.

The most important of the early British works on the history of accounting. Still very useful though obviously dated in many respects. The appendices include a chronological list of printed books on bookkeeping, 1494-1800; and a list of deceased Scottish accountants, with notes. Reprinted, London: Frank Cass and co., ltd., 1968.

See item 320.

160 HUNTER, Alexander T. 1905

The 'Unispect' system of bookkeeping. 2nd.ed. Edinburgh: Gordon Wilson, 1905.

11p. 25cm.

160 HUNTER, Alexander T. (cont.) 1905

The 'Unispect' system of bookkeeping.

REF: -

LOC. NLS; BM.

A system for "the smaller Retail Tradesman".

161 MAXWELL, John T. 1905

A Handbook to parish council finance, accounting and audit, with exemplification of the new abstract of accounts. Edinburgh: William Green and sons, 1905.

xiv,195p. 19cm.

REF: -

LOC: GUL; GP; BM.

Includes extracts from the author's article on Local Authorities' Accounts (Scotland) in the Encyclopaedia of Accounting (item 152).

162 MILLAR, Thomas John. 1905

Building society finance and statistics ... Edinburgh: T. & T. Clark, 1905.

viii,102p. 23cm.

REF: -

LOC: E; NLS; BM.

Millar was auditor of the Improved Edinburgh Property Investment Building Society and a lecturer at the Heriot-Watt College.

163 MUNRO, Andrew. 1905

Bookkeeping down to date ... Glasgow: W. & R. Holmes, (1905-6). (Not seen)

REF: -

LOC: BM.

164 COOK, Kenneth. 1906

Brewery accounts. A lecture delivered at a meeting of the Liverpool C.A.S.A. on Thursday 16th Nov., 1905. Edinburgh: William Blackwood and sons, 1906.

20p. 22cm.

REF: -

LOC: E.

A lecture given by an English Chartered Accountant to the Liverpool Chartered Accountants' Students' Association. Concludes with some lines by C.S. Calverley:

He that would shine and petrify his tutor,
Should drink draught Allsopp in its native pewter.

165 MILLAR, Thomas John. 1906

Note on the principles of bookkeeping and modern methods applied to lawyers' transactions. Edinburgh: George Waterston and sons, 1906.

30p. 14cm.

REF: -

LOC: SE; E; NLS; BM.

165 MILLAR, Thomas John. (cont.) 1906

Note on the principles of bookkeeping ...

A pocket guide for lawyers, stressing the usefulness of loose-leaf account books. The title on the cover is "Modern Bookkeeping Methods for Lawyers".

166 ANDERSON, J.W. 1907

Brown's ship's accounts and captain's letterwriter, also how to calculate exchange at foreign ports ... Glasgow: James Brown and son, 1907.

117p. 23cm.

REF: -

LOC: GP; E; NLS; BM.

------another edition. Glasgow: 1919.

LOC: NLS.

A practical guide for shipmasters.

167 MILLAR, Thomas John. 1907

Check numbers and other aids to balancing books of account. Edinburgh: George Waterston and sons, 1907.

xii,79p. 17cm.

REF: -

LOC: SE; E; NLS; BM.

168 NICOL, William Smith. 1907

Fluctuations in security values ... Inaugural address to the Insurance and Actuarial Society, Glasgow. Reprint from the Transactions, 1907.

(Not seen)

REF: -

LOC: BM.

169 MARTIN, James. 1908

The Accountant squabble: the government and the 'C.A.' case. Were the law courts bribed? A scathing exposure. Glasgow: Robert W. Pre, 1908.

28p. 18cm.

REF: -

LOC: GUL; SE.

Begins "Anyone in the Court of Session, in the month of May, 1893, must have witnessed a strange sight - five Judges of the Court throttling a hapless defender, while three bodies of Chartered Accountants rifled his pockets" and continues in the same vein. See also items 136, 139, 142, 143.

170 MUIR, Arthur H. 1909

Check figure systems ... a paper read before the Belfast Society of Chartered Accountants ... Edinburgh: W. Blackwood and sons, 1909.

16p.

(Not seen)

REF: -

LOC: BM.

171 MILLAR, Thomas John. 1910

Management bookkeeping ... Edinburgh: George Waterston and sons, 1910.

xv,114p. 19cm.

REF: -

LOC: SE; GP; E.

Describes a method designed to record "business transactions in a manner informative and intelligible to the ordinary business man". Includes an interesting appendix on "The Theory of Double Entry Examined with Reference to Method of Statement of Accounts".

The book contains an advertisement for a cumbersome, but intricate, calculating machine turned by a handle (illustrated). It was called an arithmometer.

172 BRUCE, Charles Ross. 1911

Marine engineering estimates and costs ... Glasgow: Fraser, Asher and co., 1911.

126p. 19cm.

REF: -

LOC: SE; NLS.

Bruce was an engineer. His intention was "to provide a link between the technical and commercial departments of a marine engineering establishment" (p.5). He believed that every contract passing through the works should bear its "correct proportion" of establishment charges (p.49).

173 LISLE, George and MIDDLETON, William Aberdein. 1911

Account-keeping in principle and practice. Edinburgh: William Green and sons, 1911.

xv,242p. 22cm.

REF: -

LOC: SE; GP; E; NLS; BM.

A competent text book, including material on branch accounts, costing, partnerships, companies and income tax. Both authors were C.A.s and lecturers at the Heriot-Watt College, Edinburgh.

174 MacKAY, John D.C. 1911

Company accounting. Formation to balance sheet. Glasgow: David Robertson and co., 1911.

63p. 22cm.

REF: -

LOC: NLS; BM.

-----2nd.ed. Edinburgh: 1919.

86p. 22cm.

LOC: E.

A series of worked examples.

175 MUNRO, Andrew. 1911

Elementary bookkeeping for day and evening schools and commercial classes ... 2nd.ed. Glasgow: W. & R. Holmes, (1911).

(Not seen)

REF: -

LOC: BM.

176 GREIG, William M. 1912

Greig's accounting accuracy table and bank cheque code. Aberdeen: (1912).

(Not seen)

REF: -

LOC: BM.

177 M'KIE, David. 1912

Banking and commercial arithmetic. Edinburgh: Andrew Baxendine, 1912.

155p.

(Not seen - reviewed Acc. Mag., v.16(1912)p263-4)

REF: -

LOC: BM.

178 NEAL, 1912

Neal's synopsis of bookkeeping. Edinburgh: Paddie, Ewen and co., (1912).

89p.

(Not seen - reference BM Subject Index 1916-1920)

REF: -

LOC: BM.

179 GREIG, William M. 1913

Explanation of Greig's accounting accuracy table and bank cheque code. Aberdeen: George Robb, (1913).

59p.

(Not seen)

REF: -

LOC: BM.

180 BOOKKEEPING for farmers. 1916

Edinburgh: W. Green and son, (1916).

43p. 25cm.

REF: -

LOC: NLS; BM.

The introduction claims that the "revolutionary changes brought about by the Finance Act, 1915, Session 2, in the mode of assessing farmers with Income Tax have made it imperative for farmers in their own interest to give more attention to the keeping of accounts". Consists of examples of forms.

181 MILLAR, Thomas John. 1916

Business fact classified v. double entry. The main consideration in bookkeeping, with notes on use of original documents to save labour in bookkeeping. Reprint from The Accountants' Magazine. Edinburgh and London: W. Blackwood and son, 1916.

19p. 22cm.

REF: -

LOC: GUL; NLS.

A discussion of the imperfections of contemporary double entry bookkeeping.

182 PRICE, W.M. 1916

Farm bookkeeping and accounts. Glasgow: Scottish Agricultural publishing co., 1916.

(Not seen - reference, review Acc. Mag., v.20 (1916) p.219-220.)

REF: -

LOC: -

183 MacDONALD, D.G. and GRANT, James. 1918

A Simple system of bookkeeping for farmers and small-holders with model statement of accounts and balance sheet. Edinburgh and London: W. & R. Chambers, 1918.

72p. 20cm.

REF: -

LOC: NLS; BM.

Stresses the implications for farmers of recent changes in income tax (cf. 180 above).

184 ROBERTSON, William A. and FISHER, Allan. 1919

Odd time tables. Edinburgh: Oliver and Boyd, 1919.

(Not seen - NLS copy missing since 1952)

REF: -

LOC: BM.

Source: reviewed Acc. Mag., v.23 (1919) p.504; which explains these are tables for calculating proportions of annual payments for short periods. It says "To the accountant, this book will be extremely useful".

185 SCOTT, Robert. 1919

Scott's new bookkeeping guide. Glasgow: David Robertson and co., 1919.

(Not seen)

REF: -

LOC: BM.

186 CHARTERED ACCOUNTANTS' STUDENTS' SOCIETY OF EDINBURGH and GLASGOW CHARTERED ACCOUNTANTS' STUDENTS' SOCIETY. 1920

Joint transactions. v.1 (1919-20) - v.29 (1956-58) except 1941-44. Normally annual.

APPENDIX TO PART I

The following were advertised in other books, but no copy or other reference to them has been found.

186.1 HILL, John. pre-1762

Arithmetic, both in theory and practice ... 10th.ed. Edinburgh: for Alex. Donaldson.

187 MORRISON, Charles.

The Elements of practical arithmetic simplified. (Advertised in item 63, 6th.ed., 1838)

188 MORRISON, Charles.
The General accountant.
(Advertised in item 63, 6th.ed., 1838.)

188.1 MANUAL OF COMMERCE.
Edinburgh: Oliver & Boyd, c. 1878.
(Advertised in Edinburgh Almanack, 1878.)

189 MacGREGOR, William.
MacGregor's interest tables for current accounts and discounts on bills at 18 different rates from 1 to 10 per cent.
(Advertised in item 116.)

190 M'KIE, David.
Income tax tables.
(Advertised in item 154; reviewed in Acc. Mag., v.4 (1900) p.323.)

191 M'KIE, David.
Simple interest tables.
(Advertised in item 154.)

192 LISLE, George.
Income tax tables.
(Mentioned on the title page of item 129.)

PART II: TRANSGRIPTIONS OF ACCOUNTS

Part II is arranged chronologically by date of commencement of the account. The locations given are not necessarily complete.

(i) Books

193 THE EXCHEQUER ROLLS OF SCOTLAND, (1264-1600). 1264

v.1 1264-1359 Edited by John Stuart and George Burnett.
clxxxiv,720p. 27cm. pub. 1878.
v.2 1359-1379 cxxvi,697p. 27cm. pub. 1878.
v.3 1379-1406 cvi,779p. 27cm. pub. 1880.
v.4 1406-1436 ccxii,782p. 27cm. pub. 1880.
v.5 1437-1454 cix,792p. 27cm. pub. 1882.
v.6 1455-1460 cxlviii,783p. 27cm. pub. 1883.
v.7 1460-1469 lxviii,774p. 27cm. pub. 1884.
v.8 1470-1479 lxxxviii,741p. 27cm. pub. 1885.
v.9 1480-1487 and addenda 1437-1487.
lxxvi,848p. 27cm. pub. 1886.
v.10 1488-1496 lxviii,921p. 27cm. pub. 1887.
v.11 1497-1501 lxxi,604p. 27cm. pub. 1888.
v.12 1502-1507 lxviii,889p. 27cm. pub. 1889.
vv.2-12 all edited by George Burnett.
v.13 1508-1513 edited by George Burnett and A.J.G. MacKay.
cxci,796p. 27cm. pub.1891.
v.14 1513-1522 edited by A.J.G. MacKay.
cxciii,836p. 27cm. pub. 1893.
v.15 1523-1529 lxxvii,830p. 27cm. pub. 1895.
v.16 1529-1536 lii,738p. 27cm. pub. 1897.
v.17 1537-1542 lv,947p. 27cm. pub. 1897.
v.18 1543-1556 lxxv,777p. 27cm. pub. 1898.
v.19 1557-1567 lxxiii,677p. 27cm. pub. 1898.
v.20 1568-1579 lxiv,685p. 27cm. pub. 1899.
v.21 1580-1588 lxvii,748p. 27cm. pub. 1901.
v.22 1589-1594 liii,675p. 27cm. pub. 1903.
v.23 1595-1600 lvii,601p. 27cm. pub. 1908.
vv.15-23 all edited by George Powell McNeill.

All volumes published in Edinburgh: H.M. General Register House.
LOC: GP.

194 INVENTORIES AND ACCOUNT ROLLS, 1311-1430. 1311

(in - The Correspondence, Inventories, Account Rolls and Law Proceedings of the Priory of Coldingham. London and Edinburgh: for the Surtees Society, 1841. 23cm. p.i-civ (appendix))
LOC: EUL; GUL; AUL; GP; NLS; BM.

195 THE ACCOUNTS OF THE GREAT CHAMBERLAINS OF SCOTLAND 1326

and other officials of the Crown, rendered at the Exchequer (1326-1453). Edited by Thomas Thomson. Edinburgh: for the Bannatyne Club, 1871(-45).
3v. (xviii,543,1; viii,679,xxxix; xii,576,1)p. 29cm.
(Publications of the Bannatyne Club, v.79)
LOC: EUL; GUL; AUL; GP; NLS; BM.

196 ACCOUNTS OF THE CHAMBERLAINS OF SCOTLAND 1329
in the years 1329, 1330 and 1331. From the originals in the Exchequer. With some other curious papers. (Edited by John Davidson). Edinburgh: A. Murray and J. Cochran, 1771.
iv,31p. 26cm.
LOC: SE; EUL; NLS.

197 ACCOUNTS OF SIR WILLIAM TRUSSELL. 1346
(in - Miscellany of the Scottish History Society, 9th volume. Edinburgh: T. & A. Constable for the Society, 1958. 23cm. p.9-33.
(Publications of the Scot. Hist. Soc., ser.3, v.50))
LOC: EUL; GUL; AUL; GP; NLS; BM.

The accounts arose from the keep of David II, whilst a prisoner in England.

198 EXTRACTS FROM THE ACCOUNTS OF THE BURGH OF ABERDEEN. 1398
Accounts of the Provost and Baillies, 1398-1648.
The Treasurers' accounts, 1559-1645.
(in - The Miscellany of the Spalding Club, volume 5th. Aberdeen: William Bennett for the Spalding Club, 1852. 26cm. p.39-181.)
LOC: EUL; GUL; AUL; GP; NLS; BM.

199 RENTAL BOOK OF THE CISTERCIAN ABBEY OF COUPAR-ANGUS 1443
with the breviary of the Register. Edited by the Rev. Charles Rogers. London: for the Grampian Club, 1879.
lvi,372p. 24cm.
LOC: GUL; AUL; GP.

200 ACCOUNTS OF THE LORD HIGH TREASURER OF SCOTLAND. (1473-1574). 1473

v.1	1473-1498	edited by Thomas Dickson.		
		xxxv,548p.	26cm.	pub. 1877.
v.2	1500-1504	603p.	26cm.	pub. 1900.
v.3	1506-1507	530p.	26cm.	pub. 1901.
v.4	1507-1513	692p.	26cm.	pub. 1902.
v.5	1515-1531	592p.	26cm.	pub. 1903.
v.6	1531-1538	lxxxi,613+14p.	26cm.	pub. 1905.
v.7	1538-1541	lii,627p.	26cm.	pub. 1907.
v.8	1541-1546	lxxix,624p.	26cm.	pub. 1908.
v.9	1546-1551	lxviii,599p.	26cm.	pub. 1911.
v.10	1551-1559	lxxxv,572p.	26cm.	pub. 1913.
v.11	1559-1566	lxxx,683p.	26cm.	pub. 1916.

vv.2-11 all edited by Sir James Balfour Paul.
vv.1- 9 published Edinburgh: H.M. General Register House.
vv.10-11 published Edinburgh: H.M.S.O.

cont. as:
ACCOUNTS OF THE TREASURER OF SCOTLAND.
v.12 1566-1574 edited by Charles Thorpe McInnes.
529p. 28cm. Edinburgh: H.M.S.O., 1970.
LOC: AUL; NLS.

201 LEDGER OF ANDREW HALYBURTON ... 1492-1503, 1492
together with the book of customs and valuation of merchandises in Scotland, 1612. Published by authority of the Lords of the Treasury under the direction of the Lord Clerk-Register of Scotland. (Edited by Cosmo Innes). Edinburgh: H.M. General Register House, 1867. See item 253.
cxvi,403p. illus. 27cm.
LOC: SE; AUL; E; NLS; BM.

202 ACCOUNTS OF SIR DUNCAN FORESTAR OF SKIPINCH, 1495
Comptroller, 1495-1499. (Introduction by P. Gouldensbrough). (in - Miscellany of the Scottish History Society, 9th volume. Edinburgh: T. & A. Constable for the Society, 1958. 23cm. p.57-81. (Publications of the Scot. Hist. Soc., ser.3, v.50))
LOC: EUL; GUL; AUL; GP; NLS; BM.

203 RENTALE DUNKELDENSE 1505
being the accounts of the Bishopric (A.D. 1505-1517) with Myln's "Lives of the Bishops" (A.D. 1483-1517). Translated and edited by Robert Kerr Hannay with a note on the Cathedral Church by F.C. Eeles. Edinburgh: T. & A. Constable for the Scottish History Society, 1915.
xliv,414p. 23cm.
(Publications of the Scot. Hist. Soc., ser.2, v.10)
LOC: EUL; GUL; AUL; GP; NLS; BM.

204 RENTAL BOOK OF THE DIOCESE OF GLASGOW, 1509-1570. 1509
(in - Diocesan Registers of Glasgow. Edited by Joseph Bain and Charles Rogers. London: for the Grampian Club, 1875. 2v. 24cm. v.1. p.1-265)
LOC: GUL; AUL.

204.1 MAUCHLINE ACCOUNT BOOKS OF MELROSE ABBEY, 1527-1528. 1527
Margaret H.B. Sanderson. Ayr: Ayrshire Archaeological and Natural History Society, 1975.
24p. 22cm.
Ayrshire Collections vol.11 no.5.
REF: -
LOC: SE.

205 ACCOUNTS OF THE MASTER OF WORKS 1529
for building and repairing royal palaces and castles. v.1. 1529-1615. Edited by Henry M. Paton. Edinburgh: H.M.S.O., 1957.
lxviii,423p. 25cm.
(No more published)
LOC: GP; NLS; BM.

206 AYR BURGH ACCOUNTS, 1534-1624. 1534
Transcribed and edited with an introduction, by G.S. Pryde. Edinburgh: T. & A. Constable for the Scottish History Society, 1938.
cxxv,313p. 23cm.
(Publications of the Scot. Hist. Soc., ser.3, v.28)
LOC: EUL; GUL; AUL; GP; NLS; BM.

207 RENTALE SANCTI ANDREE 1538

being the Chamberlain and Granitar accounts of the archbishopric in the time of Cardinal Betoun, 1538-1548. Translated and edited by Robert Kerr Hannay. Edinburgh: T. & A. Constable for the Scottish History Society, 1913.

lviii,246p. 23cm.

(Publications of the Scot. Hist. Soc., ser.2, v.4)

LOC: EUL; GUL; AUL; GP; NLS; BM.

208 ACCOUNTS OF THE KING'S PURSEMASTER, 1539-1540. 1539

Edited by Athol L. Murray.

(in - Miscellany ten. Edinburgh: T. & A. Constable for the Scottish History Society, 1965. 23cm. p.11-51.

(Publications of the Scot. Hist. Soc., ser.4, v.2))

LOC: EUL; GUL; AUL; GP; NLS; BM.

209 RENTAL OF THE PREBENDARY OF THE ALTAR OF ST. MARY 1543

in the collegiate church of St. Andrews, c.1543.

(in - Charters and documents relating to the burgh of Peebles with extracts from the records of the burgh, AD 1165-1710. Edinburgh: for the Scottish Burgh Records Society, 1872. 27cm. p.405-407).

LOC: SE; AUL; BM.

210 EDINBURGH RECORDS. THE BURGH ACCOUNTS. 1544

v.1. Baillies accounts, 1544-1566; Town treasurers' accounts, 1552-1567. v.2. Dean of Guild's accounts, 1552-1567. Edited by Robert Adam. Edinburgh: Colston and Coy for the Lord Provost, Magistrates and Council, 1899.

2v. (xxx,533; xiv,254)p. Facsim. 26cm.

LOC: SE; NLS; BM.

211 EXTRACTS FROM THE ACCOUNTS OF THE BURGH OF EDINBURGH, 1552-1556. 1552

(in - Extracts from the records of the burgh of Edinburgh 1528-1557. Edinburgh: for the Scottish Burgh Records Society, 1871. 27cm. p.269-369).

LOC: SE; AUL; BM.

The accounts are those of the Town Treasurers and the Deans of Guild (see item 210 above).

212 EXTRACTS FROM THE ACCOUNTS OF THE BURGH OF PEEBLES, 1554-1665. 1554

(in - Charters and documents relating to the burgh of Peebles with extracts from the records of the burgh, 1165-1710. Edinburgh: for the Scottish Burgh Records Society, 1872. 27cm. p.410-424).

LOC: SE; AUL; BM.

cont. as: Extracts from the accounts of the burgh Treasurers, 1651-1665.

(in - Extracts from the records of the burgh of Peebles, 1652-1714. Glasgow: for the Scottish Burgh Records Society, 1910. 27cm. p.191-203).

LOC: AUL; BM.

213 EXTRACTS FROM THE ACCOUNTS OF THE COMMON GOOD OF VARIOUS BURGHS 1557

in Scotland, relative to the payments for schools and schoolmasters, between the years 1557 and 1634.

(in - Miscellany of the Maitland Club, volume 2, part 1. Edinburgh: for the Maitland Club, 1840 29cm. p.39-50).

LOC: EUL; GUL; AUL; GP; NLS; BM.

214 ACCOUNTS OF THE COLLECTORS OF THIRDS OF BENEFICES, 1561-1572. 1561
Edited by Gordon Donaldson. Edinburgh: T. & A. Constable for the Scottish History Society, 1949.
xli,335p. 23cm.
(Publications of the Scot. Hist. Soc., ser.3, v.42)
LOC: EUL; GUL; AUL; GP; NLS; BM.

215 EXTRACTS FROM THE ACCOUNTS OF THE BURGH OF GLASGOW, 1573-1714. 1573
(in - Extracts from the records of the burgh of Glasgow.)
AD 1573-1643 pub. 1876. 27cm. p.445-484 (accounts 1573-1641)
AD 1630-1662 pub. 1891. 27cm. p.501-552 (accounts 1630-1662)
AD 1663-1690 pub. 1905. 27cm. p.481-524 (accounts 1662-1690)
AD 1691-1717 pub. 1908. 27cm. p.637-648 (accounts 1713-1714)

cont. as:
(Accounts of the Treasurer of the Burgh of Glasgow.)
AD 1739-1759 pub. 1911. 27cm. p.559-573 (accounts 1752,53,57,58)
all published Glasgow: for the Scottish Burgh Records Society.
LOC: SE (first two); AUL; BM.

216 PORTIONS OF RENTALS, ... HOUSEHOLD BOOKS AND INVENTORIES 1582
of Breadlebane. (1582-1626)
(in - The Blackbook of Taymouth, with other papers from the Breadlebane Charter Room. Edinburgh: for the Bannatyne Club, 1855. 29cm. (actual printed area: 17cm) p.263-351.
(Publications of the Bannatyne Club, v.100))
LOC: EUL; GUL; AUL; GP; NLS; BM.

217 THE COMPTE BUIK OF DAVID WEDDERBURNE, 1587
merchant of Dundee, 1587-1630. Edited, with an introduction, by Alexander Hastie Millar. Edinburgh: T. & A. Constable for the Scottish History Society, 1898.
lxxii,323p. 23cm.
(Publications of the Scot. Hist. Soc., v.28)
LOC: SE; EUL; GUL; AUL; GP; NLS; BM.

218 RENTALL OF THE BURGH AND CITY, 1590. (Glasgow) 1590
(in - Extracts from the records of the burgh of Glasgow, AD 1663-1690. Glasgow: for the Scottish Burgh Records Society, 1905. 27cm. p.527-534).
LOC: AUL; BM.

219 ABERDEEN SHORE WORKS ACCOUNTS, 1596-1670. 1596
Transcribed and edited by ... Louise B. Taylor. Aberdeen: the University Press, 1972.
x,668,(6)p. (1 fold.) illus. facsim. maps. 26cm.
LOC: AUL; GP.

220 EXCERPTS FROM THE BURGH ACCOUNTS 1600-1745. (Irvine) 1600
(in - Muniments of the Royal Burgh of Irvine, volume II. Edinburgh: for the Ayrshire and Galloway Archaeological Society, 1891. 29cm. p.239-335).
LOC: AUL.

221 HOUSEHOLD ACCOUNTS OF LUDOVICK, DUKE OF LENNOX; 1607
when commissioner to the Parliament of Scotland, 1607.
(in - Miscellany of the Maitland Club, volume 1. Edinburgh: for the Maitland Club, 1834. 29cm. p.159-191.
(Publications of the Maitland Club, v.25))
LOC: EUL; GUL; AUL; GP; NLS; BM.

222 RENTALS OF STRATHAVON (1608-1809) 1608
(in - The Lordship of Strathavon. Tomintoul under the Gordons, by Victor Gaffney. Aberdeen: for the Third Spalding Club, 1960. 25cm. p.190-281 (appendix 1)).
LOC: EUL; GUL; AUL; GP; NLS; BM.

223 DUMBARTON COMMON GOOD ACCOUNTS, 1614-1660. 1614
Edited by Fergus Roberts and I.M.M. Macphail. Dumbarton: the Lennox Herald, 1972.
xxi,312p. 22cm.
LOC: GP.

224 THE COMPT OF JAMES MURRAY OF KILBERTOUN, 1628
Maister of Wark to our Soverane Lord of the haill expenssis maid upoun building and reparatiounes within and about His Majesties Castell of Stirling, 1628-1629.
(in - Miscellany of the Maitland Club, volume 3, part 2. Edinburgh: for the Maitland Club, 1843. 29cm. p.365-377.
(Publications of the Maitland Club, v.57))
LOC: EUL; GUL; AUL; GP; NLS; BM.

225 THE BOOK OF ANNUALRENTARIS AND WEDSETTARIS 1633
within the Schirrefdome of Abirdein, 1633.
(in - The Miscellany of the Spalding Club, volume third. Aberdeen: William Bennett for the Spalding Club, 1846. 25cm. p.71-139).
LOC: EUL; GUL; AUL; GP; NLS; BM.

226 EXTRACTS FROM THE ACCOUNTS OF THE BURGH OF STIRLING, 1634-1752. 1634
(in - Extracts from the records of the Burgh of Stirling, AD 1667-1752. Glasgow: for the Glasgow Stirlingshire and Sons of the Rock Society, 1889. 27cm. p.299-369 (appendix)).
LOC: SE; AUL; BM.

227 CHAMBERLAIN'S ACCOUNT, 1650, DUNNOTTAR. 1650
(in - The Miscellany of the Third Spalding Club, volume II. Aberdeen: University Press for the Third Spalding Club, 1940. 25cm. p.183-210).
LOC: EUL; GUL; AUL; GP; NLS; BM.

228 RENTAL OF THE FEUDUTIES AND ANNUALRENTS 1657
payable to the burgh of Glasgow, c.1657.
(in - Extracts from the records of the burgh of Glasgow, AD 1663-1690. Glasgow: for the Scottish Burgh Records Society, 1905. 27cm. p.535-554).
LOC: AUL; BM.

229 EXTRACTS FROM THE ACCOUNT BOOK, FOR THE YEAR 1659, of Nicol Gairdiner, Treasurer of the burgh of Linlithgow. 1659

(in - Analecta Scotica - collections illustrative of the civil ecclesiastical and literary history of Scotland, chiefly from original MSS. (Edited by James Maidment.) Edinburgh: Thomas G. Stevenson, 1834. 2v. 22cm. v.1. p.204-209).

LOC: EUL; GP; BM.

230 EXCERPTS FROM THE HOUSEHOLD BOOK OF MY LORD ARCHBISHOP of St. Andrews from 1663-1666. 1663

(in - Miscellany of the Maitland Club, volume 2, part 2. Edinburgh: for the Maitland Club, 1840. 29cm. p.497-541.

(Publications of the Maitland Club, v.51))

LOC: EUL; GUL; AUL; GP; NLS; BM.

231 A KING'S COLLEGE DINNER ACCOUNT OF 1670. 1670

(in - The Miscellany of the Third Spalding Club, volume II. Aberdeen: University Press for the Third Spalding Club, 1940. 25cm. p.256).

LOC: EUL; GUL; AUL; GP; NLS; BM.

232 ACCOUNT BOOK OF SIR JOHN FOULIS OF RAVELSTON, 1671-1707. 1671

Edited by Rev. A.W. Cornelius Hallen. Edinburgh: T. & A. Constable for the Scottish History Society, 1894.

lxxiv,500p. 23cm.

(Publications of the Scot. Hist. Soc., v.16)

LOC: EUL; GUL; AUL; GP; NLS; BM.

233 THE DIARY AND GENERAL EXPENDITURE BOOK OF WILLIAM CUNNINGHAM of Craigends, ... kept chiefly from 1673-1680. Edited by Rev. James Dodds. Edinburgh: T. & A. Constable for the Scottish History Society, 1887. 1673

xliv,150p. 23cm.

(Publications of the Scot. Hist. Soc., v.2)

LOC: EUL; GUL; AUL; GP; NLS; BM.

234 THE RECORDS OF A SCOTTISH CLOTH MANUFACTORY at New Mills, Haddingtonshire, 1681-1703. Edited, ... with an introduction and notes, by W.R. Scott. Edinburgh: T. & A. Constable for the Scottish History Society, 1905. 1681

xci,366p. 23cm.

(Publications of the Scot. Hist. Soc., v.46)

LOC: EUL; GUL; AUL; GP; NLS; BM.

234.1 REVENUE OF THE SCOTTISH CROWN 1681 1681

Sir William Purves. Edited by D. Murray Rose. Edinburgh: William Blackwood and Sons, 1897.

lii,201p. 26cm.

An enquiry by one of Charles II's Solicitor-Generals for Scotland into the condition of Crown revenue.

235 THE HOUSEHOLD BOOK OF LADY GRISELL BAILLIE, 1692-1733. 1692

Edited, with notes and introduction, by Robert Scott-Moncrieff. Edinburgh: T. & A. Constable for the Scottish History Society, 1911.

lxxx,443p. illus. 23cm.

(Publications of the Scot. Hist. Soc., ser.2, v.1)

LOC: EUL; GUL; AUL; GP; NLS; BM.

236 ACCOMPT, TOUN OF GLASGOW WITH FRANCIS STEVENSON, WRIGHT, 1703-1712. 1703
(in - Extracts from the records of the burgh of Glasgow, AD 1691-1717. Glasgow: for the Scottish Burgh Records Society, 1908. 27cm. p.662-676).
LOC: AUL; BM.

237 ACCOUNT OF THE COLLECTOR OF TIENDS, 1703-7. 1703
(in - Extracts from the records of the burgh of Glasgow, AD 1691-1717. Glasgow: for the Scottish Burgh Records Society, 1908. 27cm. p.649-661).
LOC: AUL; BM.

238 MacNEILL OF CARSKEY, HIS ESTATE JOURNAL, 1703-1743. 1703
Verbatim extracts from the original manuscript. Edited, with an introduction, ... by Frank Forbes MacKay. Edinburgh: M. MacDonald, 1955.
123p. illus. 26cm.
LOC: NLS; BM.

239 ACCOUNT OF PAMPHLETS SINCE JUNE 1, 1704. 1704
(in - Analecta Scotica - collections illustrative of the civil, ecclesiastical and literary history of Scotland, chiefly from the original MSS. (Edited by James Maidment.) Edinburgh: Thomas G. Stevenson, 1837. 22cm. 2v. v.2. p.73-76).
LOC: EUL; GP; BM.

This is an account rendered to the purchaser of the pamphlets.

240 SELECTIONS FROM THE MONYMUSK PAPERS (1713-1755). 1713
transcribed and edited by Henry Hamilton. Edinburgh: T. & A. Constable for the Scottish History Society, 1945.
lxxx,255p. 23cm.
(Publications of the Scot. Hist. Soc., ser.3, v.39)
LOC: EUL; GUL; AUL; GP; NLS; BM.

241 ACCOMPT OF EXPENSES IN EDINBURGH BY ALEXANDER ROSE ... 1715. 1715
Edited, ... with an introduction by A.H. Millar.
(in - Miscellany (first volume). Edinburgh: T. & A. Constable for the Scottish History Society, 1893. 23cm. p.495-504.
(Publications of the Scot. Hist. Soc., v.15))
LOC: EUL; GUL; AUL; GP; NLS; BM.

242 LIFE AND LABOUR ON AN ABERDEENSHIRE ESTATE, 1735-1750. 1735
being selections from the Monymusk papers. Transcribed and edited by Henry Hamilton. Aberdeen: University Press for the Third Spalding Club, 1946.
xl,184p. 25cm.
LOC: EUL; GUL; AUL; GP; NLS; BM.

The accounts are transcribed on pages 1-63.

243 POWIS PAPERS, 1507-1894. 1736
Edited with an introduction by John George Burnett. Aberdeen: the Central Press for the Third Spalding Club, 1951.
(8),398p. 25cm.
LOC: EUL; GUL; AUL; GP; NLS; BM.

Accounts and estate vouchers, 1736-1834, from p.260.

244 OCHTERTYRE HOUSE BOOK OF ACCOMPTS, 1737-1739. 1737
Edited, with an introduction ..., by James Colville. Edinburgh: T. & A. Constable for the Scottish History Society, 1907.
lii,259p. 23cm.
(Publications of the Scot. Hist. Soc., v.55)
LOC: EUL; GUL; AUL; GP; NLS; BM; SE.

245 THE LOCHARKAIG TREASURE 1746
edited by Marion F. Hamilton.
(in - Miscellany (seventh volume). Edinburgh: T. & A. Constable for the Scottish History Society, 1941. 23cm. p.131-168.
(Publications of the Scot. Hist. Soc., ser.3, v.35))
LOC: EUL; GUL; AUL; GP; NLS; BM.

Consists of four documents, all with accounts relating to the investigation into this treasure.

246 THE LORDSHIP OF PAISLEY, BEING THE ACCOMPT ... 1757
for the years 1757, 1758, 1759 and 1760. Edited, with an introduction, ..., by W.M. Metcalfe. Paisley: Alexander Gardner, 1912.
lxxii,91p. 23cm.
LOC: SE; AUL; GP.

247 ACCOUNT FOR BUILDING A NEW ROAD ON TYREBAGGER HILL, 1759-60. 1759
Edited by James Cruikshank.
(in - The Miscellany of the Third Spalding Club, volume II. Aberdeen: University Press for the Third Spalding Club, 1940. 25cm. p.247-255. illus.)
LOC: EUL; GUL; AUL; GP; NLS; BM.

248 JAMES BEATTIE'S DAY BOOK, 1773-1798. 1773
Edited by Ralph S. Walker. Aberdeen: University Press for the Third Spalding Club, 1948.
vii,227p. 25cm.
LOC: EUL; GUL; AUL; GP; NLS; BM.

249 ESTIMATE FOR MAKING A CANAL. 1785
(in - An Account of the present state of the Hebrides and Western coasts of Scotland ... being the substance of a report to the Lords of the Treasury ... (by) James Anderson. Edinburgh: for C. Elliot, 1785. 22cm. p.378-385, 394-402. (Appendices 5 and 7))
LOC: GP.

The two estimates refer to what are now the Caledonian and the Crinan canals.

250 DUNCAN DEWAR. A STUDENT OF ST. ANDREWS 100 YEARS AGO. HIS ACCOUNTS. 1820
Commentary by the late Sir Peter Redford Scott Lang. Introduction by the Hon. Lord Sands. Glasgow: Jackson, Wylie and co., 1926.
xvi,190p. illus. 19cm.
LOC: NLS; BM.

(ii) Periodical Articles.

251 A MEDIEVAL SCOTS MERCHANTS' HANDBOOK. 1400
Alison Hanham. Scot. Hist. Rev. v.50 (1971) p.107-120.

Describes a manuscript in the Advocates Library (now NLS) which is in two parts, the first religious, the second a ready reckoner which includes weights and measures.

252 AYR BURGH ACCOUNTS, 1428-1429. 1428
George S. Pryde. Scot. Hist. Rev. v.31 (1952) p.139-146.

252.1 THE CUSTOMS ACCOUNTS OF KIRKCUDBRIGHT, WIGTOWN AND DUMFRIES, 1434-1560. 1434
Athol L. Murray. Trans. Dum. & Gall. N.H. & Antiq. Soc. v.40 (1963) p. 136-162.

253 HALYBURTON'S LEDGER AND HIS TIMES. 1492
F.A. Ritson. Acc. Mag. v.70 (1966) p.124-133.
See item 201.

254 THE REVENUES OF THE BISHOPRIC OF MORAY IN 1538. 1538
Athol L. Murray. Innes Review. v.19 (1968) p.40-56.

An introduction to the accounts for the year is given, followed by a transcription in Latin.

255 A DUMFRIES RENTAL. 1548
G.W. Shirley. Trans. Dum. & Gall.N.H. & Antiq. Soc. v.39 (1960-61) p.50-79.

256 THE CUSTOMS ACCOUNTS OF DUMFRIES AND KIRKCUDBRIGHT, 1560-1660. 1560
Athol L. Murray. Trans. Dum. & Gall. N.H. & Antiq. Soc. v.42 (1965) p.114-132.

A discussion of the state of custom and trade at the time is followed by a reproduction of the accounts, p. 125-132.

257 A HADDINGTON SURGEON'S ACCOUNT, 1611. 1611
Scot. Hist. Rev. v.2 (1904) p.102.

A reproduction, half a page, of the account rendered for attending the head injuries of a falconer.

258 ACCOUNTS OF THE ROYAL BURGH OF DUMFRIES, 1633-4, 1634-5, 1636-8, 1638-9. 1633
R.C. Reid. Trans. Dum. & Gall. N.H. & Antiq. Soc. v.3 (1914-15) p.291-344.

259 AN EAST LOTHIAN EXECUTOR'S ACCOUNTS, 1645-1650. 1645
A. Montgomerie. Scot. Hist. Rev. v.30 (1971) p.144-153.

260 ACCOUNT OF THE LOSSES OF THE BURGH OF DUNBAR, 1651. 1651
F.F. Roberts. Trans. East Loth. Antiq. & F.N. Soc. v.11 (1968) p.1-11.

The account refers to costs incurred by the burgh and its inhabitants whilst quartering the English army under Cromwell.

261 DAME ERSKINE'S ACCOUNT BOOK - HOUSE-KEEPING ACCOUNTS. 1674
N.N.Q. or Scot. Antiq. v.2 (1887) p.175-179.
Scot. Antiq. or N.N.Q. v.9 (1894) p.105-109; 186.

262 THE ACCOUNTS OF ST. SALVATOR'S COLLEGE, ST. ANDREWS, 1679
comprising the ordinary revenue and expenditure, the casual and contingent profits, etc., from 1679-1689, and details of the revenue of 1691.
David Hay Fleming. Proc. Soc. Antiq. Scot. v.56 (1922) p.325-350.

263 THE ACCOUNTS OF DR. ALEXANDER SKENE, PROVOST OF ST. SALVATOR'S COLLEGE, 1683
St. Andrews, relating to the extensive repairs to the college buildings, the church and the steeple, 1683-1690.
David Hay Fleming. Proc. Soc. Antiq. Scot. v.54 (1919-20) p.216-248.

264 AN EDINBURGH ACCOUNT BOOK OF TWO HUNDRED YEARS AGO. 1699
J.G.A. Baird. Scot. Hist. Rev. v.6 (1909) p.140-149.

265 AESCULAPIUS IN FIFE: A STUDY OF THE EARLY EIGHTEENTH CENTURY. 1710
Bruce Seton. Scot. Hist. Rev. v.19 (1922) p.180-189.

Describes three domestic accounts concerning two doctors, Robert Scott and Archibald Arnott.

266 LIFE IN A COUNTRY MANSE ABOUT 1720. 1711
Henry Grey Graham. Scot. Hist. Rev. v.1. (1904) p.159-172.

Describes details of pocket book of James Laurie, minister of Kirkmichael, which he kept from 1711-1732. Examples of his accounts are given, but no transcription.

267 HARRIS ESTATE PAPERS, 1724-1797.
Alick Morrison. Trans. Gael. Soc. Inverness v.45 (1967-68) p.33-97.

A long discussion on the estate and rents, followed by a transcription of the rents and accounts, p.64-97.

268 A ROXBURGHSHIRE MANSION AND ITS CONTENTS IN 1729. 1729
Alexander O. Curle. Scot. Hist. Rev. v.5 (1908) p.265-272.

Discusses and gives examples of the accounts of rents, etc., kept by the factor of the estate, Archibald Jerdon.

269 AN EIGHTEENTH CENTURY HAWICK FARMER'S RENT AND STIPEND BOOK, 1730-73. 1730
R.E. Scott. Trans. Hawick Arch. Soc. (1963) p.36-40.

270 TWO EIGHTEENTH CENTURY TAILORS. 1732
Stuart Maxwell. Trans. Hawick Arch. Soc. (1972) (reprint available)

271 EDINBURGH TREASURER'S ACCOUNTS, 1734-35. 1734
Scot. Antiq. or N.N.Q. v.12 (1897) p.25-29.

272 A DRUMLANRIG ESTATE BOOK, 1740-1745. 1740
R.C. Reid. Trans. Dum. & Gall. N.H. & Antiq. Soc. v.18 (1931-33) p.85-97.

The estate book consists of the accounts of the chamberlains and agents, some of which are transcribed, p.89-97.

273 THE RECONSTRUCTION OF BRAEMAR AND COGARFF CASTLES, 1746. 1748
John Malcolm Bulloch. Proc. Soc. Antiq. Scot. v.65 (1930-31) p.379-381.

Despite the date given in the title, the account runs from 1748-1750.

274 THE DAY BOOKS OF A DUMFRIESSHIRE DRAPER, 1810-1838. 1810
W.A.J. Prevost. Trans. Dum. & Gall. N.H. & Antiq. Soc. v.33 (1954-55) p.48-57.

275 AN OLD DAY BOOK 1814
John Byers. Trans. Hawick Arch. Soc. (1959) p.14-18.

Random extracts from the daybook of David and John Ballantyne of Shaws, in Liddesdale.

PART III: HISTORY OF SCOTTISH ACCOUNTING

Part III (i) and (ii) are arranged chronologically by date of publication of the book or article. All early volumes of accounting journals contain articles that are now of historical interest.

(i) Books

276 CLERK, Sir John and SCROPE, John. 1820

The Forms and powers of the Court of the Exchequer in Scotland, to which is added an appendix containing the rules of procedure and certain minutes of Court relating thereto. Edinburgh: J. Hay and co., 1820.

vii,343p. 32cm.

The manuscript was compiled whilst the two authors were Barons of Exchequer, from 1708 to 1724. The appendix was updated from time to time until publication in 1820.

277 McCLELLAND, James. 1869

The Origin and present organisation of the profession of Chartered Accountancy in Scotland. Glasgow: 1869.

See items 106 and 315.

277.1 COUPER, Charles Tennant. 1879

Report of the trial ... against the Directors and Manager of The City of Glasgow Bank. Edinburgh: The Edinburgh Publishing Company, 1879.

viii,476p. 25cm.

REF: -

LOC: SE; NLS; BM.

See items 279.1 and 309.3.

278 CHARTERED ACCOUNTANTS OF SCOTLAND 1896

Official directory.

Published annually except: 1916-17, 1941-47 and 1949-50, no edition published; and 1919-1932, when it was biennial.

The Chartered Accountants of Scotland comprised the Society of Accountants in Edinburgh, the Institute of Accountants and Actuaries in Glasgow, and the Society of Accountants in Aberdeen. The publication was continued by The Institute of Chartered Accountants of Scotland.

279 BROWN, Richard. 1905

A History of accounting and accountants. Edinburgh: 1905.

See items 159 and 320.

-----Reprinted, London: Frank Cass and co., ltd., 1968.

279.1 WALLACE, William (editor). 1905

Trial of the City of Glasgow Bank Directors, edited by William Wallace. Glasgow and Edinburgh: (1905).

viii,472p. plates. 23cm.

REF: -

LOC: SE; NLS; BM.

See items 277.1 and 309.3.

280 MURRAY, David. 1930

Chapters in the history of bookkeeping, accountancy and commercial arithmetic. Glasgow: Jackson, Wylie and co., 1930.

vi,519p. 24cm.

Scotland is dealt with specifically on p.1-122 and 308-350. <u>See</u> also items 293 and 321, and Addenda.

281 WILSON, Duncan K. 1935

The History of mathematical teaching in Scotland to the end of the eighteenth century. London: the University Press, 1935.

vi,99p. 23cm.

282 COOPER BROTHERS AND CO. 1954

A History of Cooper Brothers and co., 1854-1954. London: published privately, 1954.

xv,116p. illus. 25cm.

283 INSTITUTE OF CHARTERED ACCOUNTANTS OF SCOTLAND, The. 1954

A History of the Chartered Accountants of Scotland from earliest times to 1954, written and published on the occasion of the centenary of the Institute. Edinburgh: W. Blackwood and sons, for the Institute, 1954.

xii,183p. 29 plates. 26cm.

<u>See</u> item 307.

284 YAMEY, B.S. 1962

Some topics in the history of financial accounting in England, 1500-1900.

(<u>in</u> - Studies in accounting theory. Edited by W.T. Baxter and Sidney Davidson. London: Sweet and Maxwell, 1962. 26cm. p.14-43.)

Includes several references to books and accounts from Scotland.

285 YAMEY, B.S., EDEY, H.C. and THOMSON, H.W. 1963

Accounting in England and Scotland, 1543-1800. London: Sweet and Maxwell, 1963.

xi,228p. 25cm.

286 LAW, Alexander. 1965

Education in Edinburgh in the eighteenth century. London: the University Press, 1965.

239p. 23cm.

See in particular p.168-173 and 204-207, for bookkeeping and mathematics.

287 WILSON, STIRLING AND CO. 1964

Wilson, Stirling and co., 1864-1964. Published privately, 1964.

14p. illus. 22cm.

288 MANN, JUDD, GORDON AND CO. 1967

Interim account of a going concern. Some essays in the history of the firm of Mann, Judd, Gordon and co., Chartered Accountants, Glasgow, <u>circa</u> 1817 to 1967, on the occasion of the 150th. anniversary of its foundation. Published privately, 1967.

58p. illus. 21cm.

289 KIDSTON, JACKSON AND CO. 1969

The Antecedents of Kidston, Jackson and co. Published privately, 1969.

12p. 21cm.

(Type-written format)

290 PARKER, R.H. 1969

The Origins of the break-even chart: Sir John Mann.

(in - Management accounting: an historical perspective. London: Macmillan, 1969. 23cm. p.65-66.)

290.1 MURRAY, Athol L. 1971

Sir John Skene and the Exchequer, 1594-1612

(in - Miscellany One by various authors. Edinburgh: The Stair Society, v.26, 1971. 26cm. p.125-155)

290.2 ZEFF, Stephen A. 1972

Activities of the Scottish Institute.

(in - his Forging Accounting Principles in Five Countries: A History and an Analysis of Trends. Champaign, Ill: Stipes Publishing Company, 1972. 23cm. p.50-57)

Traces the development of the research effort of The Institute of Chartered Accountants of Scotland.

290.3 MURRAY, Athol L. 1973

The pre-Union records of the Scottish Exchequer.

(in - Prisca Munimenta edited by Felicity Ranger. London: University of London Press, 1973. 25cm. p.169-183)

A comprehensive discussion originally published in Journal of the Society of Archivists v.2 (1961)

(ii) Periodical Articles

291 HOWDEN, James. 1894
The Profession in Scotland: a retrospect.
Acc. (1894) p.646-652. and Trans. C.A. Stud. Soc. Edin. v.6 (1893-94) p.7-30.

292 CAMPBELL, (Provost). 1897
The Presidential address to the summer conference ... of the Scottish Institute of Accountants.
Acc. v.23 (1897) p.631-632.

A brief résumé of the history of the Institute and the profession in Scotland.

293 MURRAY, David. 1905
Bookkeeping and accountancy: Scottish practice in the 17th and 18th centuries.
Acc. v.32 (1905) p.356-360. (From the Glasgow Herald, March 14th, 1905.)

This article forms the basis of the first part of his book, item 280. See also item 321, and Addenda.

294 LAIRD, T.P. 1919
The Development of accountancy in relation to commerce.
Acc. Mag. v.23 (1919) p.458-471.

Inaugural lecture of the Professor-elect of Accounting and Business Method at Edinburgh University. Starts from Italy and Pacioli, but concentrates on Scotland.

295 AN EIGHTEENTH CENTURY AUDIT. 1923
J.Acc. v.36 (1923) p.282-3.

Copy of a letter "Direction for examining the account of Auchinleck", dated 4th August, 1792, with comments.

295.1 EDWARDS, Ronald S. 1937
Some notes on the early literature and development of cost accounting in Great Britain - III.
Acc. v.97 (1937) p.253-5.

Mainly a discussion of the cost accounting aspects of Robert Hamilton's Introduction to Merchandise (see item 40 above). Reproduces Hamilton's "Field Book" from the 2nd edition (1788).

296 BROWNING, Robert. 1954
The Chartered Accountants of Scotland, 1854-1954.
Acc. Mag. v.58 (1954) p.453-465.

297 MANN, Sir John. 1954
Glimpses of early accountancy in Glasgow.
Acc. Mag. v.58 (1954) p.297-306.

298 ARMET, H. 1956
Mr. Treasurer, Edinburgh - before 1835.
Loc. Gov. Fin. v.60 (1956) p.140-2, 169-70.

299 STEPS IN THE EVOLUTION OF THE PROFESSION IN THE UNITED KINGDOM. 1957
Acc. v.137 (1957) p.544-5.

Lists the important dates from 1853, when the founder members of the Society of Accountants in Edinburgh first met, until 1957, when the Society of Incorporated Accountants and Auditors was integrated with the three Chartered Institutes.

300 THE GLASGOW STAFF OF THE ROYAL BANK A CENTURY AND HALF AGO. 1959
The Three Banks Review (1959) p.27-35.

300.1 MURRAY, Athol L. 1960
Exchequer and Council in the reign of James V. Juridical Review N.S. v.5 (1960) p.209-225.

301 MURRAY, Athol L. 1961
The Procedure of the Scottish Exchequer in the early eighteenth century.
Scot. Hist. Rev. v.40 (1961) p.89-117.

Describes the work of the accountants and Lord Auditors, the layout of the Rolls and some examples of entries from the Rolls are given.

302 McBAIN, A.G. 1964
218 St. Vincent Street, Glasgow: the Institute's Glasgow premises.
Acc. Mag. v.68 (1964) p.509-520.

A history of the building and its previous occupants. See item 323.

303 MITCHELL, J.F. 1965
Accountants of Excise.
Acc. Mag. v.69 (1965) p.246-247.

Discusses the people who worked in the Scottish Excise.

303.1 DUNLOP, Anna B.G. 1965
Scottish chartered accountants
The Scottish Genealogist v.12 (May 1965) p.12-22.

303.2 MURRAY, Athol L. 1965
The Scottish Treasury, 1667-1708.
Scot. Hist. Rev. v.45 (1965) p.89-104.

304 DUNLOP, Anna B.G. 1966
Chartered Accountants'Hall, Edinburgh.
Acc. Mag. v.70 (1966) p.478-483, 541-547, 640-643, 710-714, 803-808.

The history and architecture of the buildings which now comprise the Hall are described and illustrated.

305 PARKER, R.H. 1966
Three topics in the history of accounting.
Acc. v.154 (1966) p.218-222.

The second and third topics, "Professional Accountancy" and "Accounting education and the universities" discuss development in Scotland as well as elsewhere.

306 DUNLOP, Anna B.G. 1967
Accountants' clubs.
Acc. Mag. v.71 (1967) p.116-121.

Discusses the history and membership of three Scottish clubs, two nineteenth and one twentieth century.

307 SINCE 1954. 1968
Acc. Mag. v.72 (1968) p.427-432.

Continues item 283 up to 1968, a year at a time.

308 HISTORICAL ACCOUNTING 1970
Acc. v.162 (1970) p.920-921.

Brief history of the North of Scotland Fire and Life Assurance company, with a reproduction of the accounts of the first year of trading.

309 MURRAY, Athol L. 1973
The Comptroller, 1425-1488.
Scot. Hist. Rev. v.52 (1973) p.1-29.

Describes the work involved in the post, and gives some of the items of accounts.

309.1 PARKER, R.H. 1974
The First Scottish book on accounting.
Acc. Mag. v.78 (1974) p.358-361.

A reprint of Professor Parker's article on Robert Colinson: Idea Rationaria. See appendix p.73.

309.2 STEWART, Jas. C. 1974
Qualification for membership a hundred years ago.
Acc. Mag. v.78 (1974) p.263-265.

309.3 TYSON, R.E. 1974
The Failure of the City of Glasgow Bank and the rise of independent auditing.
Acc. Mag. v.78 (1974) p.126-131.
See items 277.1 and 279.1.

309.4 VAMPLEW, Wray. 1974
"A Careful and Most Ingenious Fabrication of Imaginary Accounts": Scottish railway company accounts before 1868.
Acc. Mag. v.78 (1974) p.307-312.

309.5 SABINE, B.E.V. 1975
The Scandal at the Edinburgh Stamp Office.
Acc. Mag. v.79 (1975) p.253.

309.6 STEWART, Jas. C. 1975
The Emergent Professionals.
Acc. Mag. v.79 (1975) p.113-116.

309.7 MEPHAM, M.J. and STONE, W.E. Forthcoming
John Mair.
Accounting and Business Research. Forthcoming.
See items 19 and 37.

(iii) Biographies

Part III (iii) is arranged chronologically by date of death of the subject, followed by the autobiography of the living subject. For further information on Scottish accountants reference could be made to the obituaries of The Accountant's Magazine.

310 BORTHWICK, Archibald. (Eminent accountants of the past, no.1) 1863
Acc. Mag. v.1 (1897) p.148-155.

311 BROWN, James. (Eminent accountants of the past, no.6) 1864
Acc. Mag. v.4 (1900) p.85-90.

312 BALFOUR, Robert. (Eminent accountants of the past, no.7) 1869
Acc. Mag. v.5 (1901) p.94-106.

313 CHRISTIE, Robert. (Eminent accountants of the past, no. 5) 1869
Acc. Mag. v.3 (1899) p.356-358.

314 LINDSAY, Donald. (Eminent accountants of the past, no.3) 1876
Acc. Mag. v.1 (1897) p.495-499.

315 M'CLELLAND, James. (Eminent accountants of the past, no.2) 1879
Acc. Mag. v.1 (1897) p.294-300. See item 106.

316 ROBERTSON, Alexander Weir. (Eminent accountants of the past, no.9) 1879
Acc. Mag. v.8 (1904) p.295-297.

317 PEARSON, Charles. (Eminent accountants of the past, no.4) 1884
Acc. Mag. v.2 (1898) p.553-554.

318 BARSTOW, Charles Murray. (Eminent accountants of the past, no.10) 1885
Acc. Mag. v.15 (1911) p.289-291.

319 MESTON, James. (Eminent accountants of the past, no.8) 1892
Acc. Mag. v.7 (1903) p.196-200. See item 113.

320 BROWN, Richard. 1918
Richard Brown, President of the Society of Accountants in Edinburgh.
Acc. Mag. v.22 (1918) p.279-286. See item 159.

321 MURRAY, David. 1928
David Murray - accounting historian, 1842-1928. E. Stevelinck.
Acc. Mag. v.76 (1972) p.393-396. See items 280 and 293.

322 YOUNG, Arthur. 1948
Arthur Young and the business he founded. New York: published privately, 1948.
71p. portrait. 23cm.

323 McBAIN, A.G. 1967
1912 et seq. - a personal interim report.
Acc. Mag. v.71 (1967) p.220-225.

An autobiographical article which throws light on professional practice from 1912. See item 302.

IDEA RATIONARIA,

OR

THE PERFECT ACCOMPTANT,

Necessary for all Merchants and Trafficquers;

CONTAINING

THE TRUE FORME OF *BOOK-KEEPING*,

According to the *Italian* Methode:

Wherein is First,

The Introduction to the Forme,

244. *Queries* and *Answers*, with Instructions how to Ballance the *Leger*, two *Waste-Books* transported in two *Journals*, out of which are transported 2. *Legers* both Ballanced.

After which followes

A MONETH-BOOK,
INVOYS-BOOK,
FACTOR-BOOK,
SPECIE or CASH-BOOK;
Instructions how to keep a Book of Petty-Charges *or* Pocket-Book.

By ROBERT COLINSON.

EDINBURGH,

Printed by DAVID LINDSAY, Mr. JAMES KNIBLO, JOSUA van SOLINGEN and JOHN COLMAR, in the Year 1683.

Title page of Robert Colinson:
Idea rationaria, or, the Perfect accomptant ...
Edinburgh, 1683 (see item 1)

APPENDIX: ROBERT COLINSON'S IDEA RATIONARIA

by R.H. Parker*

The 1680s were an important decade in Scottish history. Scots law was presented as a complete and coherent system for the first time, in Stair's Institutes, published in 1681. The deposition of James VII and II in 1688 marked the effective end of a dynasty which had ruled Scotland since 1371. In the religious settlement that followed, presbyterianism was firmly established.

It was during this same decade, in 1683, that the first Scottish book on accounting was published, nearly two centuries after Pacioli's Summa of 1494 and 140 years after the first book in the English language, Hugh Oldcastle's A briefe instruction and maner how to keepe bookes of Accompts ... of 1543. The long delay reflects the relatively under-developed state of the Scottish economy and the ready availability of textbooks from south of the Border.

By 1683 there was, as J. Row Fogo observed, "no particular merit ... in producing a good work on book-keeping"[1]. Robert Colinson's Idea Rationaria is, however, "sensible and reasonably straightforward"[2] and for this reason, as well as for its chronological importance in the history of accounting in Scotland, it is worth a short article. The practices recommended in it are typical of their time and show interesting variations from those of the present.

The Book

The title page is reproduced opposite. Note the reference to the "Italian Methode", as double-entry bookkeeping was still commonly called; the method of teaching by "Queries and Answers" which is characteristic of the period; and the names of the recommended books of account.

The arrangement of Colinson's book is as follows:-

(a) Title page (see reproduction)

(b) Dedication to the Honourable Mr. James Kennedy, "Lord Conservator of the Priviledges of the Scots Nation in the 17. Provinces of the Nether-lands, and his Majesties Resident there, for all affaires of his Majesties ancient Kingdom of Scotland, &c."

* Professor Parker is indebted to Professor B.S. Yamey, of the London School of Economics, and Professor T.A. Lee, of Edinburgh University, for their comments on a previous draft.

(c) Two laudatory poems by Mr. Ninian Paterson and Mr. J. Kniblo. These are of no great literary merit, but Professor Yamey regards them as one of the attractions of the book to present-day readers.[3] Elsewhere[4] he has considered at length the strength of Paterson's claim for double-entry, that:-

This was the fam'd, and quick invention, which
Made Venice, Genoa, and Florence rich:

(d) Table of Contents

(e) A letter to the "Merchants in Edinburgh, And all other Lovers of this Profitable Science".

(f) Thirty-one pages describing the "Convenience" of bookkeeping; the various books of account Colinson deems it necessary to keep: Waste Book, Journal, Ledger, Factor Book ("to place down what is sent you by others, to dispose of the charges and sales"), Invoice Book, Month Book ("which tells you what summes you are to pay every moneth in the year, and day when, and who is to pay you"), Book of Petty Charges, Specie or Cash Book (necessary where more than one currency is dealt in: Row Fogo points out that, in addition to the national coinage, which was very bad, there were large quantities of foreign money in circulation, particularly English and Dutch), Copy Book of Letters; and 244 questions and answers to "find out the right Debitor and Creditor upon all the Posts[5] of the Wast-Book, when you transport them to the Journal, and first of placing down the Inventar of the Stock". The questions and answers are interrupted between nos. 138 and 139 for a brief instruction (not in question and answer form) on balancing accounts, transferring them to a new book and on "companies-accompts" (i.e. partnership accounts).

(g) Two specimen sets of books (waste-book, journal and ledger).

The Author

Who was Colinson? Both Paterson and Kniblo refer to him as "Captain". He tells us that he has been "both a Student and Practitioner (of commerce) now these 25 years". It is clear from several references that, like many Scottish merchants of his time, he had lived and traded in the Low Countries. The title of his book is in Latin; his only quotation in a foreign language is in Dutch.

The Rules

The usual method of expounding the rules of double entry in British textbooks on bookkeeping up to the 18th century was "to present a great mass of rules applicable to the particular cases of a large variety of transactions",[6] to do so by means of a series of questions and to follow this by a specimen set of books. Some, but not all, authors also included a general rule. Occasionally this was in verse. Dafforne, for example, the only British author on bookkeeping to whom Colinson refers, wrote as follows in "The Merchant's Mirrour"[7]:-

The Ower, or the Owing thing,
Or what-so-ever comes to thee:
Upon the Left-hand see thou bring;
For there the same must placed bee.

But they unto whom thou doest owe;
Upon the Right let them bee set;
Or what-so-ere doth from thee goe,
To place them there doe not forget.

Colinson fortunately does not break into verse, but neither does he, regrettably, include a general rule. Instead, he immediately plunges into detail. Here are the first three questions and answers:-

(1) Q. What make you Debitor for the first branch of your Stock (i.e. Capital) which is ready money?

A. Cash Debitor to my Stock, for so much as I have in at the beginning. This word Cash is used now generally for money Accompts, it comes from the Italian word Cassa, which is a money Chest, or the like, which keeps it; therefore you Charge it Debitor for what is in't.

(2) Q. What is Debitor for the several Marchandize that you have lying by you unsold?

A. Such goods, naming them in your Journal, or as many of them as you will keep a particular Accompt of, Charging every one by itself Debitor, to Stock for the whole value it cost, with the Charges it hath cost since bought.

(3) Q. What is Debitor for your houses?

A. Such a house called so and so, every one of them what they stand me Debitor to Stock for all Charges, and Reparations to this day.

Specimen Accounts

In connection with this last entry some contemporary writers recommended the inclusion of both private and business assets in the accounts. Colinson

F. 15		*Edinburgh, Anno* 1682.				
		PROFITE and LOSS, Debet.				
Febr.	14	To *Thomas Trader*	4	4	—	—
	—	To Cash for rebate to *James Trusty*	1	4	—	—
Mar.	29	To *Thomas Factor* my accompt Currant for rebate	18	8	14	2
June	9	To Cash for rebate	23	3	—	—
	29	To Cash payed for House-hold expence and servants wages	23	130	—	—
	30	To several accompts lost on them as *per* Journal	..	253	5	4
	—	To Stock for the neat gain	1	103	11	—
		Summa	L	506	10	6

Colinson is quite clear about the necessity to separate business and private assets:-

> Now I say, a man may have a private stock which he will conceal, and a stock in trade [i.e. business assets] also; but then he must bring none of his private stock into his trading stocks Books, lest he confuse himself. Wherein can this private stock consist? it must be in Lands, Houses, Rents, Jewels, and House furnishing, &c. for which private stock let him keep a Book, which he may easily do apart. [page 5]

In the specimen sets of books, however, Colinson includes household expense and servants' wages, and wagers (see above). Perhaps he regarded the last as a business transaction!

The accounts in the two specimen ledgers show a number of interesting variations from 20th-century practice. The Profit and Loss Account in the first ledger is reproduced above.

The first thing to notice is the absence of any reference to sales, purchases and opening and closing stocks of goods. Instead we have, <u>via</u> two entries in the journal, two items of £386.16.0[8] and £253.5.4 summarising the gains and losses on various accounts. £35.5.0, for example, is lost upon "Wines of France", that account being debited for the cost of wine bought, £430.0.0, and charges, £6.15.0, and credited with various sales amounting in all to £472.0.0. A separate column is used to record volume in "Tuns" with a loss of half a tun "in lackage".

Edinburgh, Anno 1682.

PROFITE and LOSS, Credite.

Febr.	16	*Per George Dane*	5	3	—	—
	—	*Per Alexander Norman*	5	1	10	—
June	29	*Per Cash* for Prentice-fee	23	100	—	—
	30	*Per Gilbert Callant* in *Aberdeen*	26	15	4	6
	—	*Per* several accompts for so much gained on them, as *per* Journal	—	386	16	—
		Summa	L.	506	10	6

There are similar accounts for Seck of Zeres (i.e. sherry), Iron, Mader, Indigo Lauro, Clothe, Sarges, Salmond, Herrings, Stockines, Hides, Wheat, Mum-Beer and, in the second ledger, Tallow. None of the goods accounts illustrated by Colinson has a closing balance, nor does he anywhere in his book discuss the valuation problems involved.[9] He contents himself with stating (page 20) that

> Debet side of goods Accompt is what they cost me with charges, Credit is what is sold or sent away, or otherwayes disposed of.

The gains and losses in the summarising journal entries also include:-

(a) References to a number of voyage accounts. £71.13.4, for example, is gained from a Voyage to Rotterdam in the Ship Bonaventure, goods being bought from David Mills in Aberdeen for £970 and sold by William Cornelisen in Rotterdam for £1,041.13.4.

(b) £30 "gained by wagering".

(c) Commissions received, £47.13.8.

(d) £158 "lost by insuring other mens goods".

(e) £30 "lost upon Sea hazard by Skippers".

The first four items on the debit side of the Profit and Loss Account reproduced all refer to rebates allowed; the first two items on the credit side are rebates received. The remaining items are £130 "payed for House-hold expence and servants wages"; £100 for a "Prentice-fee" (the apprenticeship was presumably for a period of years but no part of the fee is carried forward); and £15.4.6 commission received from Gilbert Callant.

The fixed asset[10] accounts, e.g. House called Black-Hall which is debited with the original cost plus reparations and rents payable and credited with rents receivable, follow what Yamey calls the arithmetical balance basis of valuation. No attempt is made to transfer revenue and expense items to the Profit/

Profit and Loss Account or to revalue the asset. The balances on such accounts are obviously rather meaningless.

The last account in each ledger is the "Ballance" account, to which are transferred all account balances still open after transfers to the Profit and Loss Account and transfer of the "neat gain" therefrom to Stock (i.e. Capital). It is in effect an unclassified Balance Sheet contained within the books of account.

REFERENCES

1 R. Brown (editor): A History of Accounting and Accountants (Edinburgh: Jack, 1905) p.155. (items 159 and 279)

2 B.S. Yamey, H.C. Edey and H.W. Thomson: Accounting in England and Scotland, 1543-1800 (London: Sweet and Maxwell, 1963) p.171. (item 285)

3 ibid

4 B.S. Yamey: "Scientific Bookkeeping and the Rise of Capitalism", Economic History Review, June 1949, reprinted in W.T. Baxter: Studies in Accounting (London: Sweet and Maxwell, 1950)

5 i.e. items. The modern French word is "poste".

6 J.G.C. Jackson: "The History of Methods of Exposition of Double-entry Book keeping in England", in A.C. Littleton and B.S. Yamey: Studies in the History of Accounting (London: Sweet and Maxwell, 1956) p.288.

7 Richard Dafforne: The Merchant's Mirrour (London, 1636) introductory pages to specimen ledger. There is a copy of this book in the Antiquarian Collection of The Institute of Chartered Accountants of Scotland.

8 The figure in the journal entry heading is actually £393.16.0, but the items in it add up to £386.16.0.

9 For a historical survey of the valuation of stock-in-trade see R.H. Parker "Lower of Cost and Market in Britain and the United States: an Historical survey", Abacus, v.1 no.2, 1965; reprinted in R.H. Parker and G.C. Harcourt (editors): Readings in the Concept and Measurement of Income (Cambridge University Press, 1969).

10 Colinson does not classify assets into groups and does not use the term "fixed asset".

INDEX TO AUTHORS

All references are made to part, date and item number. Within each author, titles are arranged alphabetically by first word not an article.
* indicates that the work is the first Scottish edition, but the book was originally published elsewhere.
≠ indicates that the date is not the earliest Scottish edition.
a indicates that the work is an article, section (ii) of Parts II or III.
b indicates that the work is biographical, section (iii) of Part III. Biographical works follow the works written by the author.

ABERDEEN			
Book of annualrentaris and wedsettaris ..., 1633.	II	1633	225
Extracts from the accounts of the burgh, 1398-1645.	II	1398	198
--- Shore works accounts, 1596-1670.	II	1596	219
ABERDEEN: Society of Accountants			
see CHARTERED ACCOUNTANTS OF SCOTLAND.	III	1896	278
------; Students.			
see MESTON, James.	I	1886	113
ABIRDEIN			
see ABERDEEN.			
ACCOUNTANT (pseud.)			
Principles of life annuities and assurances ...	I	1829	77
ADAM, Robert (editor)			
Edinburgh records. The burgh accounts. (1544-1567)	II	1544	210
ALLAN, Alexander			
see HARDIE, William and ALLAN, Alexander	I	1893≠	127
ALLAN, F.H.			
see M'KIE, David, 4th.ed. 1918.	I	1900	150
ALLEN, George.			
Allen's forty lessons in practical double entry book-keeping ...	I	1885	110
ANDERSON, J.W.			
Brown's ship's accounts and captain's letter writer, ...	I	1907	166
ANDERSON, James (editor)			
Estimate for making a canal.	II	1785	249
ANONYMOUS			
Bookkeeping for farmers ...	I	1916	180
Dame Erskine's account book - house keeping accounts.	IIa	1674	261
Edinburgh Treasurer's accounts, 1734-1735.	IIa	1734	271
Eighteenth century audit, An.	IIIa	1923	295
Elements of bookkeeping in a series of short examples.	I	1864	102.1
Glasgow staff of the Royal Bank a century and a half ago.	IIIa	1959	300
Haddington surgeon's account, 1611, A.	IIa	1611	257
Historical accounting.	IIIa	1970	308
Manual of commerce.	I	app	188.1
Merchant's and Banker's commercial pocket guide.	I	c.1845	89.2
Pleasing art of money-catching.	I	1840	85.2
Since 1954.	IIIa	1968	307
Steps in the evolution of the profession ...	IIIa	1957	299
ARMET, H.			
Mr.Treasurer, Edinburgh - before 1835.	IIIa	1956	298

ATTFIELD, J.H.			
see BOGAL, John D.S. and ATTFIELD, J.H.	I	1895	135
AYR			
Burgh accounts, 1428-1429.	IIa	1428	252
Burgh accounts, 1534-1624.	II	1534	206
BAILLIE, *Lady* Grisell			
Household book of ---, 1692-1733.	II	1692	235
BAIN, Joseph and ROGERS, Charles.			
Rental book of the diocese of Glasgow, 1509-1570.	II	1509	204
BAIRD, J.G.A.			
Edinburgh account book of two hundred years ago, An.	IIa	1699	264
BALFOUR, Robert.			
Eminent accountants of the past, no.7.	IIIb	1869	312
BARNETSON, James.			
McDougall's exercises in bookkeeping.	I	1899	146
BARSTOW, Charles Murray.			
Eminent accountants of the past, no.10.	IIIb	1885	318
BEATTIE, James.			
---'s Day book, 1773-1798.	II	1773	248
BELL, John.			
Chambers's examination book-keeping ...	I	1889	117
Examination questions in bookkeeping by double entry ...	I	1867	105
BLACKWOOD (William) and SONS (Publishers).			
Accountant's Magazine, The.	I	1897	140
BOAZ, James.			
Interval tables, interest tables, ...	I	1820	66
--- and JAFFRAY, William.			
Interest tables at 4%.	I	1823	71
BOGAL, John Douglas Stewart and ATTFIELD, J.H.			
M'Dougall's bookkeeping for elementary schools ...	I	1895	135
BORTHWICK, Archibald.			
Eminent accountants of the past, no.1.	IIIb	1863	310
BRAEMAR			
Reconstruction of --- and Cogarff castles ...	IIa	1748	273
BREADLEBANE			
Portions of rentals, household books and inventories ..	II	1582	216
BRODIE, David.			
Short set of bookkeeping by double entry ..., A.	I	1831	79
BROWN, George.			
Account of the rotula arithmetica ..., An.	I	1700	4
Arithmetica infinita.	I	1717	10
Compendious but a compleat system of decimal arithmetick, A.	I	1701	6
Specie book serving ... to turne any ... piece of silver...	I	1700	5
BROWN, James.			
Eminent accountants of the past, no.6.	IIIb	1864	311
BROWN, Nicol.			
Organisation of the gold mining business, ..., The.	I	1897	141
Specimens of working records and account books ...	I	1896	138
BROWN, Richard.			
History of accounting and accountants, A.	(I	1905	159
	(III	1905	279
Richard Brown, president of the Society of Accountantants ...	IIIb	1918	320

BROWN, Robert.			
Book of the landed estate ..., The.	I	1869	105.2
BROWNE, George.			
see BROWN, George.			
BROWNING, Robert.			
Chartered Accountants of Scotland, The, 1854-1954.	IIIa	1954	296
BRUCE, Charles Ross.			
Marine engineering estimates and costs ...	I	1911	172
BRYCE, J.			
Treatise on bookkeeping by double and single entry ...	I	1860+	97
BUCHANAN, Colin.			
Engraved system of bookkeeping, An.	I	1808	57
Practical book-keeping ...	I	1806	54
Writingmaster and accountant's assistant ..., The.	I	1798	49
BULLOCH, John Malcolm.			
Reconstruction of Braemar and Cogarff castles, 1746.	IIa	1748	273
BURNETT, George (editor)			
Exchequer Rolls of Scotland, The.	II	1264	193
BURNETT, John George (editor)			
Powis papers, 1507-1894.	II	1736	243
BUTTERWORTH AND SON (Publishers)			
Butterworth's young arithmeticians instructor ...	I	1805	53
BYERS, John.			
Old day-book, An.	IIa	1814	275
CALCULATOR (pseud.)			
Counting-house manual ... outline of practical book-keeping	I	1843	89
CAMPBELL, -			
Presidential address to the summer conference ...	IIIa	1897	292
CARTER, F. Hayne.			
Practical bookkeeping adapted to commercial and judicial accounting ...	I	1861	99
CARTER, Fred. W.			
see CARTER, F.H. 6th.ed. 1890.	I	1861	99
CHAMBERLAIN (of Dunnottar).			
--- Accounts, 1650.	II	1650	227
CHAMBERLAINS OF SCOTLAND.			
Accounts of the --- in the years 1329-1331.	II	1329	196
see also GREAT CHAMBERLAINS OF SCOTLAND.			
CHAMBERS, William and Robert (Publishers)			
Chambers' bookkeeping ...	I	1892	123
CHARTERED ACCOUNTANTS OF SCOTLAND.			
Charter of incorporation, bye-laws, rules and regulations.	I	1904	155.1
Charter of incorporation, rules, regulations and bye-laws.	I	1904	155.2
Official directory.	III	1896	278
Royal charter ... and bye-laws, rules and regulations.	I	c.1867	105.1
CHARTERED ACCOUNTANTS' STUDENTS' SOCIETY OF EDINBURGH			
Transactions.	I	1886	114
--- and GLASGOW CHARTERED ACCOUNTANTS' STUDENTS' SOCIETY Joint Transactions.	I	1920	186
CHRISTIE, Robert.			
Eminent accountants of the past, no.5.	IIIb	1869	313

CLERK, Sir John and SCROPE, John.			
Forms and powers of the Court of the Exchequer ..., The.	III	1820	276
COCKER, Edward.			
Cocker's arithmetick ... revised by George Fisher.	I	1749*	21
Cocker's arithmetic ... revised by John Mair.	I	1751*	22
COGARFF.			
Reconstruction of Braemar and --- castles ...	IIa	1748	273
COLDINGHAM PRIORY.			
Inventories and account rolls, 1311-1430.	II	1311	194
COLINSON, Robert.			
Idea rationaria.	(I	1683	1
	(Appendix		73
COLLECTOR OF TIENDS.			
Account of the ---, 1703-7. (Glasgow).	II	1703	237
COLLECTORS OF THE THIRDS OF BENEFICES.			
Accounts of the ---, 1561-1572.	II	1561	214
COLQUHOUN, James.			
Corporation finance.	I	1894	128
COLVILLE, James (editor)			
Ochertyre house book of accompts, 1737-1739.	II	1737	244
COMMISSIONERS OF NATIONAL EDUCATION.			
see IRELAND: Commissioners of National Education.	I	1863*	101
COMMON GOOD.			
Dumbarton - accounts, 1614-1660.	II	1614	223
Extracts from the accounts of --- of various burghs ...	II	1557	213
COOK, Kenneth.			
Brewery accounts.	I	1906	164
COOPER BROTHERS AND CO.			
History of ---, 1854-1954, A.	III	1954	282
COUPAR-ANGUS.			
Rental book of the Cistercian Abbey of --- ...	II	1443	199
COUPER, Charles Tennant.			
Report of the trial ... against the Directors and Manager of the City of Glasgow Bank.	III	1879	277.1
CRAIGHEAD, William.			
Arithmetic in all its parts, vulgar and decimal ...	I	1760	26
CRUIKSHANK, James (editor)			
Account for building a new road on Tyrebagger Hill, 1759-60.	II	1759	247
CUNNINGHAM, William (of Craigends)			
Diary and general expenditure book of ---, 1673-1680.	II	1673	233
CURLE, Alexander O.			
Roxburghshire mansion and its contents in 1729, A.	IIa	1729	268
DAVIDSON, John (A.M. of Burntisland)			
Young arithmetician's guide ..., The.	I	1834†	80
--- and SCOTT, Robert.			
Arithmetic modernised.	I	1827	76
DAVIDSON, John (editor)			
Accounts of the Chamberlains of Scotland ...	II	1329	196
DEFOE, Daniel.			
Complete English Tradesman, The.	I	1839*	85.1
DEWAR, Duncan.			
---. A Student of St. Andrews ... His accounts.	II	1820	250

DICKSON, Thomas (editor)			
Accounts of the Lord High Treasurer of Scotland.	II	1473	200
DOBSON, Robert.			
see GORDON, William and DOBSON, Robert.	I	1771	36
DODD, Arthur Francis.			
Railway accounts and their audit.	I	1904	156
DODDS, *Rev.* James (editor)			
Diary and general expenditure book of William Cunningham	II	1673	233
DONALDSON, Gordon (editor)			
Accounts of the collectors of the thirds of benefices ..	II	1561	214
DRUMMOND, John.			
Accomptant's pocket-companion, The: a manual ...	I	1718	11
DUMBARTON.			
--- Common good accounts, 1614-1660.	II	1614	223
DUMFRIES.			
Accounts of the treasurers of the royal burgh of ---	IIa	1633	258
Customs accounts of --- and Kirkcudbright, 1560-1660.	IIa	1560	256
DUNBAR.			
Account of losses of the burgh of ---	IIa	1651	260
DUNKELD.			
Rentale Dunkeldense, being the accounts of the bishopric ...	II	1505	203
DUNLOP, Anna B.G.			
Accountants' clubs.	IIIa	1967	306
Chartered Accountants' Hall, Edinburgh.	IIIa	1966	304
Scottish chartered accountants.	IIIa	1965	303.1
DUNN, Thomas.			
Tables of simple interest computed decimally ...	I	1821	68
DUNNOTTAR.			
Chamberlain's accounts, 1650, --- .	II	1650	227
EDEY, H.C.			
see YAMEY, B.S., EDEY, H.C. and THOMSON, H.W.	III	1963	285
EDINBURGH			
--- records. The burgh accounts. (1544-1567).	II	1544	210
Extracts from the accounts of the burgh of ---	II	1552	211
Treasurer's accounts, 1734-35.	IIa	1734	271
EDINBURGH: Chartered Accountants' Students' Society.			
Transactions.	I	1886	114
-----: General Board of Lunacy.			
Rules and forms ... keeping of the accounts ...	I	1883	108
-----: Society of Accountants.			
see CHARTERED ACCOUNTANTS OF SCOTLAND.	III	1896	278
EDWARDS, Ronald S.			
Some notes on the early literature and development of cost accounting in Great Britain - III.	IIIa	1937	295.1
ERSKINE, *Dame*.			
--- account book - house keeping accounts.	IIa	1674	261
EXCHEQUER, COURT OF.			
Forms and powers of the ---	III	1820	276
EXCHEQUER, SCOTLAND.			
--- rolls of Scotland.	II	1264	195
Procedure of the --- in the early eighteenth century.	IIIa	1961	300

FAIRBAIRN, James.			
Fairbairn's interest tables ...	I	1861	100
FARQUHARSON, Alexander.			
Rural accountant, The.	I	1813	61
FINDLATER, John.			
Bookkeeping by double entry explained.	I	1900*	149
FISHER, Allan.			
see ROBERTSON, William A. and FISHER, Allan.	I	1919	184
FISHER, George.			
Arithmetic in the most plainest and most concise methods	I	1756	23
Cocker's arithmetick ... revised by George Fisher.	I	1749*	21
Instructor, The.	I	1763	30
FLEMING, David Hay.			
Accounts of Dr. Alexander Skene ..., 1683-1690.	IIa	1683	263
Accounts of St. Salvators college, ...	IIa	1679	262
FORESTAR, Sir Duncan of Skipinch.			
Accounts of --- comptroller, 1495-1499.	II	1495	202
FOULIS, Sir John of Ravelston.			
Account book of ---, 1671-1707.	II	1671	232
GAFFNEY, Victor.			
Rentals of Strathavon.	II	1608	222
GAIRDINER, Nicol. (Treasurer of Linlithgow)			
Extracts from the account book of ---	II	1659	229
GLASGOW.			
Accompt, the toun of --- with Francis Stevenson, wright.	II	1703	236
Account of the collector of tiends, 1703-1707.	II	1703	237
Extracts from the accounts of the burgh of ---, 1573-1714.	II	1573	215
Rental book of the diocese of ---	II	1509	204
Rental of feuduties and annualrents ...	II	1657	228
Rentall of the burgh and city, 1590.	II	1590	218
GLASGOW: Institute of Accountants and Actuaries.			
see CHARTERED ACCOUNTANTS OF SCOTLAND.	III	1896	278
GLASGOW CHARTERED ACCOUNTANTS' STUDENTS' SOCIETY.			
Transactions.	I	1904	157
see also CHARTERED ACCOUNTANTS' STUDENTS SOCIETY OF EDINBURGH and GLASGOW ---	I	1920	186
GORDON, William.			
General counting-house and man of business, The.	I	1766	33
Universal accountant ..., The.	I	1763	31
--- and DOBSON, Robert.			
Elements, analysis and practice of arithmetic ... business.	I	1771	36
GOULDENSBROUGH, P. (editor)			
Accounts of Sir Duncan Forestar of Skipinch ...	II	1495	202
GRAHAM, Henry Grey.			
Life in a country manse about 1720.	IIa	1711	266
GRANT, James.			
see MacDONALD, D.G. and GRANT, James.	I	1918	183
GREAT BRITAIN: Customs.			
Instructions for the collectors... regular methods of accompting.	I	1707	7
GREAT CHAMBERLAINS OF SCOTLAND.			
Accounts of the ---, The.	II	1326	195

GREIG, William M.			
Explanation of Greig's accounting accuracy table ...	I	1913	179
Greig's accounting accuracy table ...	I	1912	176
HALBERT, William.			
Practical figurer, The.	I	1789	44
HALLEN, <u>Rev</u>. A.W. Cornelius (editor).			
Account book of Sir John Foulis of Ravelston ...	II	1671	232
HALLIDAY, J.			
Complete ready reckoner ... , The.	I	1826	74
HALYBURTON, Andrew.			
Ledger of --- , The, 1492-1503.	II	1492	201
<u>see also</u> RITSON, F.A.	IIa	1492	253
HAMILTON, Henry. (editor)			
Life and labour on an Aberdeenshire estate, 1735-1750.	II	1735	242
Selections from the Monymusk papers, 1713-1755.	II	1713	240
HAMILTON, Marion. (editor)			
Locharkaig treasure, The.	II	1746	245
HAMILTON, Robert. fl. 1727.			
Rental accounts made easy ...	I	1727	16
HAMILTON, Robert.			
Introduction to merchandise ..., An.	I	1777	40
Short system of arithmetic and bookkeeping ..., A.	I	1796+	48
HAMILTON, William.			
Bookkeeping new modelled ...	I	1735	18
HANHAM, Alison.			
Medieval Scots merchants' handbook, A, c.1400.	IIa	1400	251
HANNAY, Robert Kerr. (editor)			
Rentale Dunkeldense, being the accounts of the bishopric	II	1505	203
Rentale Sancti Andree ...	II	1538	207
HARDIE, William.			
Manual of bookkeeping for law agents ...	I	1893	126
--- and ALLAN, Alexander.			
Manual of bookkeeping by double entry ...	I	1893+	127
HARRIS			
--- estate papers, 1724-1797.	IIa	1724	267
HAY FLEMING, David.			
<u>see</u> FLEMING, David Hay.			
HENDERSON, Richard.			
Young estate managers guide, The.	I	1898	144
HERIOT, Alexander.			
Book containing tables for finding out the exchange of money and annualrents ..., A.	I	1697	3
HILL, John.			
Arithmetic both in theory and practice ...	I	1765*	32
Arithmetic both in theory and practice.	I	app	186.1
HINES, G., JONES, B. and PUMPHREY, H.			
Easy bookkeeping for small co-operative societies ...	I	1887	115
HOWARD, C. Frusher.			
Howard's Anglo-American art of reckoning.	I	1888*	115.1
HOWATT, John.			
Compendium of practical bookkeeping ..., A.	I	1842	88

HOWDEN, James.			
Profession in Scotland, The: a retrospect.	IIIa	1894	291
HUNTER, Alexander T.			
'Unispect' system of bookkeeping, The.	I	1905/	160
HUTTON, Charles.			
Complete course of bookkeeping ..., A.	I	1838	83
Complete treatise on bookkeeping, A, ... additions by J. Trotter.	I	1838*	84
Complete treatise on practical arithmetic and book-keeping, A.	I	1804*	52
INGLIS, William.			
Bookkeeping by single and double entry ...	I	1849	91
Farm bookkeeping.	I	1866	103
Single entry bookkeeping.	I	1866/	104
see also CHAMBERS, W. & R. (publishers)	I	1892	123
INGRAM, Alexander.			
Principles of arithmetic explained ..., The.	I	1826	75
see also HUTTON, Charles. revised by A. Ingram.	I	1804*	52
HUTTON, Charles. edited by A. Ingram.	I	1838*	84
MELROSE, A. (another edition) 1812.	I	1791	47
--- and TROTTER, J.			
see MELROSE, A. 26th.ed. 1853.	I	1791	47
INNES, Cosmo. (editor)			
Ledger of Andrew Halyburton, ..., The.	II	1492	201
INNES, John.			
Dissertation concerning the arithmetick of annuities ..., A.	I	1761	27
INSTITUTE OF ACCOUNTANTS AND ACTUARIES IN GLASGOW			
see CHARTERED ACCOUNTANTS OF SCOTLAND.	III	1896	278
INSTITUTE OF ACCOUNTANTS OF GLASGOW.			
Deed of constitution and rules or regulations.	I	1853	91.1
INSTITUTE OF CHARTERED ACCOUNTANTS OF SCOTLAND, The.			
History of the Chartered Accountants of Scotland ...,A.	III	1954	283
IRELAND: Commissioners of National Education.			
Elements of bookkeeping ...	I	1863*	101
IRVINE.			
Excerpts from the burgh accounts, 1600-1745.	II	1600	220
JAFFRAY, William.			
see BOAZ, James and JAFFRAY, William.	I	1823	71
JAMIESON, John.			
Easy introduction to bookkeeping ..., An.	I	1835	82
JOHNSTON, Elias.			
see HAMILTON, Robert. 1820 ed.	I	1777	40
JONES, B.			
see HINES, G., JONES, B. and PUMPHREY, H.	I	1887	115
KIDSTON, JACKSON AND COMPANY.			
Antecedents of ---, The.	III	1969	289
KING'S COLLEGE, Aberdeen.			
--- dinner account of 1670, A.	II	1670	231
KING'S PURSEMASTER.			
Accounts of the ---, 1539-1540.	II	1539	208
KIRKCUDBRIGHT.			
Customs accounts of Dumfries and ---, 1560-1660.	IIa	1560	256

LAIRD, T.P.
Development of accountancy in relation to commerce, The. IIIa 1919 294
LANG, Sir Peter Redford Scott. (editor)
Duncan Dewar. A student of St. Andrews ... His accounts. II 1820 250
LASSEN, Claudius.
Commercial guide, The: systematic book keeping ... I 1891 120
LAURIE, John.
Tables of simple and compound interest ... I 1776 39
LAW, Alexander.
Education in Edinburgh in the 18th century. III 1965 286
LESLIE, Sir John.
Philosophy of arithmetic ..., The. I 1817 64
LEYBOURN, William.
Panarithmologia. I 1761* 28
LINDSAY, Donald.
Eminent accountants of the past, no.3. IIIb 1876 314
LINLITHGOW.
Extracts from the account book ... treasurer of the burgh ... II 1659 229
LISLE, George.
Accounting in theory and practice ... I 1899 147
Deposit receipt interest tables. I 1888 116
Elementary bookkeeping. I 1894 129
Encyclopaedia of accounting. I 1903 152
Examination papers of the C.A.S. ... Board, with answers. I 1894 130
Income tax tables. I app 192
Local Government (Scotland) Act ... accounts ... County Councils I 1891 121
LISLE, George and MIDDLETON, William Aberdein.
Account-keeping in principle and practice. I 1911 173
LITTLE, Robert.
Principles of double entry bookkeeping explained ..., The. I 1903 153
LOCHARKAIG.
The --- treasure. (1746) II 1746 245
LORD HIGH TREASURER OF SCOTLAND.
Accounts of the --- (1473-1574). II 1473 200
LORRAIN, William.
Bookkeeping by double entry ... (and) single entry. I 1807 56
LUDOVICK, Duke of Lennox.
Household account of ---, ... II 1607 221
LUNACY
see EDINBURGH: General Board of Lunacy. I 1883 108
LUNDIN, Robert.
Reason for accompting by debitor and creditor ..., The. I 1718 12

McBAIN, A.G.
218 St. Vincent Street, Glasgow: ... IIIa 1964 302
1912 et seq. - a personal interim report ... IIIb 1967 323
MacCALL, John Campbell.
Art and practice of account keeping, The. I 1884 109
McCLELLAND, James.
Origin and present organisation of the profession of chartered accountancy in Scotland, The. (I 1869 106 / (III 1869 277
Eminent accountants of the past, no.2. IIIb 1879 315
M'CLYMONT, John W.
Lawyers' cash bookkeeping, ... I 1890 119

MacDONALD, D.G. and GRANT, James.			
Simple system of bookkeeping for farmers ..., A.	I	1918	183
MacGHIE, Alexander.			
Principles of bookkeeping explain'd ..., The.	I	1718	13
MacGREGOR, William.			
MacGregor's interest tables ...	I	app	189
McINNES, Charles Thorpe. (editor)			
Accounts of the treasurer of Scotland.	II	1473	200
MacKAY, A.J.G. (editor)			
Exchequer rolls of Scotland, The.	II	1264	193
MacKAY, Frank Forbes. (editor)			
MacNeill of Carskey, his estate journal, 1703-1743.	II	1703	238
MacKAY, John D.C.			
Company accounting. Formation to balance sheet.	I	1911	174
M'KIE, David.			
Bank bookkeeping.	I	1900	150
Banking and commercial arithmetic.	I	1912	177
Income tax tables.	I	app	190
Monthly interest tables at 1, 1½ and 2%.	I	1885	111
Simple interest tables.	I	app	191
Tables of compound interest and annuities ...	I	1903	154
MacLAREN, James.			
Improved system of practical book keeping ... single entry ...	I	1853+	92
Set of books adapted to MacLaren's book keeping ...	I	1853	93
MacLAUCHLAN, James John.			
On life assurance bookkeeping	I	1891	122
MacLean, John Dalziel.			
Bookkeeping as a specific subject ...	I	1892	124
Bookkeeping for the classroom and counting house ...	I	1857+	95
Introduction to counting house and examination book-keeping ...	I	1892	125
MacLEOD, John M.			
Exhibition accounts and finance ...	I	1903	154.1
MacNEILL, - (of Carskey)			
--- his estate journal, 1703-1743.	II	1703	238
McNEILL, George Powell (editor)			
Exchequer rolls of Scotland, The.	II	1264	193
MacPHAIL, I.M.M. (editor)			
see ROBERTS, Fergus and MacPHAIL, I.M.M.	II	1614	223
MAIDMENT, James (editor)			
Account of pamphlets since June 1, 1704.	II	1704	239
Extracts from the account book ... Linlithgow.	II	1659	229
MAIR, John.			
Arithmetic, rational and practical ...	I	1766	34
Bookkeeping methodiz'd.	I	1736	19
Bookkeeping moderniz'd.	I	1773	37
Cocker's arithmetic, ... revised by John Mair.	I	1751*	22
MALCOLM, Alexander.			
New treatise of arithmetic and bookkeeping ..., A.	I	1718	14
MANN, Sir John.			
Glimpses of early accountancy in Glasgow.	IIIa	1954	297

MANN, JUDD, GORDON & CO.			
Interim account of a going concern ...	III	1967	288
MARSHALL, James.			
Interest at four per cent.	I	1823	72
MARTIN, James.			
Accountant 'CA' case, The.	I	1896	139
Accountant profession, The: a public danger.	I	1895	136
Accountant squabble, The: ...	I	1908	169
Did the devil win the toss? ...	I	1897	142
Sanctification of the lie, The ...	I	1897	143
MASTERS OF WORKS.			
Accounts of the --- for building ... royal palaces ...	II	1529	205
MAXWELL, John T.			
Handbook to parish council finance, accounting ..., A.	I	1905	161
MAXWELL, Stuart.			
Two eighteenth century tailors.	IIa	1732	270
MEPHAM, J.M. and STONE, W.E.			
John Mair.	IIIa	-	309.7
MELROSE, A.			
Concise system of practical arithmetic ...	I	1791	47
MESTON, James.			
Opening address (to) the Aberdeen Accountants' Students' ...	I	1886	113
Eminent accountants of the past, no.8.	IIIb	1892	319
METCALFE, W.M. (editor)			
Lordship of Paisley, being the accompt ..., The.	II	1757	246
MIDDLETON, William Aberdein.			
see LISLE, George and MIDDLETON, William Aberdein.	I	1911	173
MILLAR, Alexander Hastie. (editor)			
Accompt of expenses in Edinburgh by Alexander Rose ...	II	1715	241
Compte buik of David Wedderburne ...	II	1587	217
MILLAR, Robert Cockburn.			
Accountants' handbook of interest states ..., The.	I	1889	118
MILLAR, Thomas H.			
Practical introduction to life and fire assurance ..., A.	I	1841	87
MILLAR, Thomas John.			
Building society finance and statistics ...	I	1905	162
Business fact classified v. double entry ...	I	1916	181
Check numbers and other aids ...	I	1907	167
Management bookkeeping.	I	1910	171
Note on the principles of bookkeeping ...	I	1906	165
MITCHELL, J.F.			
Accountants of Excise.	IIIa	1965	303
MONTGOMERIE, A.			
East Lothian executor's accounts, 1645-1650, An.	IIa	1645	259
MONTGOMERIE, Archibald.			
Bookkeeping for every business: a manual ...	I	1858	96
MONYMUSK.			
Life and labour on an Aberdeenshire estate, 1735-1750 ...	II	1735	242
Selections from the --- papers, 1713-1755.	II	1713	240
MOODY STUART, Alexander.			
see STUART, Alexander Moody.			

MORAY.			
Revenues of the bishopric of --- in 1538, The.	IIa	1538	254
MORISON, John.			
Tables of interest at 3, 4, 4½ and 5% ...	I	1789	45
MORRISON, Alick.			
Harris estate papers, 1724-1754.	IIa	1724	267
MORRISON, Charles.			
Complete system of practical bookkeeping ..., A.	I	1814	63
Elements of practical arithmetic simplified, The.	I	app	187
General accountant, The.	I	app	188
Introduction to bookkeeping and business ...	I	1819	66.1
Series of improved mercantile forms and accounts, ..., A.	I	1860	98
Young lady's guide to practical arithmetic ... accounts..	I	1820	68
MORRISON, James.			
Accomptant's guide, The. A new system of arithmetic ...	I	1801	50
Compendium of practical arithmetic ..., A.	I	1814+	64
Complete system of merchant's accounts ..., A.	I	1808	58
Complete treatise on practical bookkeeping ..., A.	I	1803	51
Elementary principles and rules of bookkeeping ...	I	1810	59
Young ladies' guide to practical arithmetic and book-keeping.	I	1813	62
MUIR, Arthur H.			
Check figure systems ...	I	1909	170
MUNRO, Andrew.			
Bookkeeping down to date ...	I	1905	163
Elementary bookkeeping for day and evening schools ...	I	1911+	175
MUNRO, Innes.			
Guide to farm-bookkeeping ..., A.	I	1821	70
MURRAY, Athol L.			
Accounts of the King's pursemaster ...	II	1539	208
Comptroller, 1425-1488, The.	IIIa	1973	309
Customs accounts of Dumfries and Kirkcudbright, 1560-1660.	IIa	1560	256
Customs accounts of Kirkcudbright, Wigtown and Dumfries, 1434-1560.	IIa	1434	252.1
Exchequer and Council in the reign of James V.	IIIa	1960	300.1
Pre-Union records of the Scottish Exchequer, The.	III	1973	290.3
Procedure of the Scottish Exchequer ..., The.	IIIa	1961	301
Revenues of the bishopric of Moray in 1538, The.	IIa	1538	254
Scottish Treasury, 1667-1708, The.	IIIa	1965	303.2
Sir John Skene and the Exchequer, 1594-1612.	III	1971	290.1
MURRAY, David.			
Bookkeeping and accountancy: Scottish practice ...	IIIa	1905	293
Chapters in the history of bookkeeping ...	III	1930	280
David Murray - accounting historian ...	IIIb	1928	321
MURRAY, James. (of Kilbertoun)			
Compte of --- Maister of Wark ... Castell of Stirling.	II	1628	224
MURRAY, Robert.			
New system of commercial arithmetic, A.	I	1830	78

NEAL, -			
Neal's synopsis of bookkeeping ...	I	1912	178
NELSON, James.			
Bookkeeping by double entry exemplified ...	I	1871	107
NEW MILLS, Haddingtonshire.			
Records of a Scottish cloth manufactory at ---	II	1681	234
NEWALL, W.			
Merchant's companion, The, ... for making up of accompts...	I	1715	9
NICOL, William Smith.			
Fluctuations in security values ...	I	1907	168
NORTON, George Pepler.			
Balancing for expert bookkeepers.	I	1894	131
OCHTERTYRE HOUSE.			
--- book of accompts, 1737-1739.	II	1737	244
PAISLEY.			
Lordship of ---, being the accompt ..., The.	II	1757	246
PARKER, R.H.			
First Scottish book on accounting, The.	IIIa	1974	309.1
Origins of the break even chart, The: Sir John Mann.	III	1969	290
Three topics in the history of accounting.	IIIa	1966	305
PATERSON, James.			
Scots arithmetician, The.	I	1685	2
PATON, Henry M. (editor)			
Accounts of the masters of works ... royal palaces ...	II	1529	205
PAUL, Sir James Balfour. (editor)			
Accounts of the Lord High Treasurer of Scotland.	II	1473	200
PEARSON, Charles.			
Eminent accountants of the past, no.4.	IIIb	1884	317
PEEBLES.			
Extracts from the accounts of the burgh of ---, 1554-1665.	II	1554	212
PERRY, William.			
Man of business and gentleman's assistant ..., The.	I	1774	38
POWIS			
--- papers, 1507-1894. (Accounts 1736)	II	1736	243
PREVOST, W.A.J.			
Day-books of a Dumfriesshire draper, The, 1810-1838.	IIa	1810	274
PRICE, W.M.			
Farm bookkeeping and accounts.	I	1916	182
PRYDE, George S. (editor)			
Ayr burgh accounts, 1428-1429.	IIa	1428	252
Ayr burgh accounts, 1534-1624.	II	1534	206
PUMPHREY, H.			
see HINES, G., JONES, B. and PUMPHREY, H.	I	1887	115
PURVES, Sir William.			
Revenue of the Scottish Crown, 1681.	II	1681	234.1

REID, R.C.			
Accounts of the treasurers of the royal burgh of Dumfries.	IIa	1633	258
Drumlanrig estate book, A, 1740-1745.	IIa	1740	272
RITSON, F.A.			
Halyburton's ledger and his times.	IIa	1492	253
ROBERTS, F.F.			
Account of the losses of the burgh of Dunbar.	IIa	1651	260
ROBERTS, Fergus and MacPHAIL, I.M.M. (editors)			
Dumbarton common good accounts, 1614-1660.	II	1614	223
ROBERTSON, Alexander Weir.			
Eminent accountants of the past, no.9.	IIIb	1879	315
ROBERTSON, J.A.			
Business of an accountant, The.	I	1895	137
ROBERTSON, William A. and FISHER, Allan.			
Odd time tables.	I	1919	184
ROGERS, Rev. Charles. (editor)			
Rental book of the Cistercian Abbey of Coupar-Angus ...	II	1443	199
see also BAIN, Joseph and ROGERS, Charles.	II	1509	204
ROSE, Alexander.			
Accompt of expenses in Edinburgh by ---	II	1715	241
ROSS, John Munn.			
Law relating to audits and auditors, The.	I	1894	132
ST. ANDREWS.			
Excerpts from the household book of my Lord Archbishop of ---	II	1663	230
Rentale Sancti Andree, being the ... accounts of the archbishopric ...	II	1538	207
---: Collegiate church.			
Rental of the Prebendary of the altar of St. Mary of ---	II	1543	209
---: St. Salvator's College.			
Accounts of --- ...	IIa	1679	262
see also	IIa	1683	263
ST. MARY, altar of.			
Rental of the Prebendary of the ---	II	1543	209
ST. SALVATOR'S COLLEGE, St. Andrews.			
Accounts of ---	IIa	1679	262
SANDERSON, Margaret H.B.			
Mauchline account books of Melrose Abbey.	II	1527	204.1
SABINE, B.E.V.			
The Scandal at the Edinburgh Stamp Office.	IIIa	1975	309.5
SANDS, Lord. (editor)			
Duncan Dewar. A student of St. Andrews ... His accounts.	II	1820	250
SCOTT, R.E.			
Eighteenth century Hawick farmer's rent and stipend book ...	IIa	1730	269
SCOTT, Robert.			
see DAVIDSON, John and SCOTT, Robert.	I	1827	76
SCOTT, Robert.			
Graphic bookkeeping exercises.	I	1903	155
New century bookkeeping for business people.	I	1901	151
Scott's new bookkeeping guide.	I	1919	185
SCOTT, William.			
New system of practical arithmetic for ... business men, A.	I	1782	41.1
SCOTT, W.R. (editor)			
Records of a Scottish cloth manufactory at New Mills ...	II	1681	234

SCOTT-MONCRIEFF, Robert. (editor)			
Household book of Lady Grisell Baillie ..., The.	II	1692	235
SCROPE, John.			
see CLERK, *Sir* John and SCROPE, John.	III	1820	276
SCRUTON, James.			
Practical counting house, The.	I	1777	41
SETON, Bruce.			
Aesculapius in Fife: ...	IIa	1710	265
SHIRLEY, G.W.			
Dumfries rental, A.	IIa	1548	255
SKENE, *Dr*. Alexander.			
Accounts of ---, provost of St. Salvator's College ...	IIa	1683	263
SMITH, James.			
Tables of annualrent or simple interest ...	I	1718	15
SMITH, John.			
On a new ... plan. Tables for calculating interest at 5% ...	I	1810	60
SMITH, Thomas.			
Tables of interest for the use of bankers and others ...	I	1785	43
SMITH NICOL, William.			
see NICOL, William Smith.			
SOCIETY OF ACCOUNTANTS IN ABERDEEN.			
see CHARTERED ACCOUNTANTS OF SCOTLAND.	III	1896	278
SOCIETY OF ACCOUNTANTS IN EDINBURGH.			
see CHARTERED ACCOUNTANTS OF SCOTLAND	III	1896	278
SOMERVILLE, J.			
Bookkeeping (by double entry) made easy.	I	1899	148
SPENCE, David.			
Arithmetick compendiz'd.	I	1714	8
STENHOUSE, William.			
Tables of simple interest and of commission ...	I	1806	55
see also MELROSE, A. 2nd.ed. 1820.	I	1791	47
STEPHENS, Henry.			
Book of the farm, The.	I	1844	89.1
STEVELINCK, E.			
David Murray, accounting historian ...	IIIb	1928	320
STEVENSON, Francis.			
Accompt, the toun of Glasgow with ---, wright.	II	1703	236
STEVENSON, William.			
Bookkeeping by double entry reduced ... to one simple rule.	I	1762	29
General discourse shewing the usefulness of the Italian method ..., A.	I	1732	17
Serious advice to tradesmen ... learning bookkeeping ..., A.	I	1756	25
STEWART, Jas. C.			
Emergent professionals, The.	IIIa	1975	309.6
Qualification for membership a hundred years ago.	IIIa	1974	309.2
STEWART, Robert.			
Practical treatise on arithmetic arranged for pupils ..., A.	I	1853/	94
Treatise on arithmetic, in theory and practice ..., A.	I	1834	81
STIRLING.			
Compte of James Murray ... Maister of Wark ... Castell of ---	II	1628	224
Extracts from the accounts of the burgh of ---	II	1634	226

STONE, W.E.			
see MEPHAM, M.J. and STONE, W.E.	IIIa	-	309.7
STRATHAVON.			
Rentals of ---	II	1608	222
STRATHIE, David.			
Fixed machinery.	I	1892	125.1
STUART, Alexander Moody.			
Bookkeeping: observations and suggestions.	I	1894	133
STUART, John. (editor)			
Exchequer rolls of Scotland, The.	II	1264	193
TAYLOR, Donald.			
Counting house manual, The.	I	1838	85
TAYLOR, Louise B. (editor)			
Aberdeen shore works accounts.	II	1596	219
TEACHER OF BOOKKEEPING (pseud.)			
see WEBSTER, William. appendix.	I	1756	25
THIRDS OF BENEFICES.			
see COLLECTORS OF THE THIRDS OF BENEFICES.	II	1561	214
THOMSON, H.W.			
see YAMEY, B.S., EDEY, H.C. and THOMSON, H.W.	III	1963	285
THOMSON, John.			
Readiest reckoner in miniature ..., The.	I	1815	65
Tables of interest at 3, 4, 4½ and 5% ...	I	1768	35
Universal calculator, The.	I	1784	42
THOMSON, Thomas. (editor)			
Accounts of the Great Chamberlains of Scotland, The.	II	1326	195
TODD, James.			
Government examination papers for leaving certificate ...	I	1894	134
TOLMIE, David.			
Elementary treatise on bookkeeping by double entry ..., An.	I	1885	112
TREASURER OF SCOTLAND.			
Accounts of the ---	II	1473	200
TROTTER, A.			
see INGRAM, Alexander. 42nd.ed. 1864.	I	1826	75
see MELROSE, A. 44th.ed. 1881.	I	1791	47
TROTTER, Alexander. (of Dreghorn)			
Method of farm-bookkeeping ..., A.	I	1825	73
TROTTER, James.			
see HUTTON, Charles. Additions by ---	I	1838*	84
see MELROSE, A. 26th.ed. 1853.	I	1791	47
TRUSSELL, Sir William.			
Accounts of ---	II	1346	197
TURNBULL, Andrew D. Lindsay.			
Some suggestions in regard to life office accounting ...	I	1898	145
TURNBULL, Andrew Hugh.			
Tables of compound interest and annuities ...	I	1863	102
TYREBAGGER HILL.			
Account for building a new road on ---, 1759-60.	II	1759	247

TYSON, R.E.			
Failure of the City of Glasgow Bank and the rise of independent auditing, The.	IIIa	1974	309.3
VAMPLEW, Wray.			
"A Careful and Most Ingenious Fabrication of Imaginary Accounts": Scottish railway accounts before 1868.	IIIa	1974	309.4
WALKER, Ralph S. (editor)			
James Beattie's day book, 1773-1798.	II	1773	248
WALLACE, Robert.			
Pocket guide to commercial bookkeeping, The.	I	1847/	90
WALLACE, William. (editor)			
Trial of the City of Glasgow Bank Directors.	III	1905	279.1
WARDHAUGH, John Broadfoot.			
Accountant's digest ..., The.	I	1904	158
WATERSTON, William.			
Manual of commerce ..., A.	I	1840	86
WEBSTER, William.			
Essays on bookkeeping ...	I	1758	27
WEDDERBURNE, David.			
Compte buik of --- ...	II	1587	217
WILSON, Duncan K.			
History of mathematical teaching in Scotland ..., The.	III	1935	281
WILSON, John.			
Introduction to arithmetick ..., An.	I	1741	21
WILSON, STIRLING AND COMPANY.			
---, 1864-1964.	III	1964	287
YAMEY, B.S.			
Some topics in the history of financial accounting ...	III	1962	284
---, EDEY, H.C. and THOMSON, H.W.			
Accounting in England and Scotland, 1543-1800.	III	1963	285
YOUNG, Arthur.			
Arthur Young and the business he founded.	IIIb	1948	322
YOUNG, David.			
Farmer's account-book of expenditure and produce ..., The.	I	1790	46
ZEFF, Stephen A.			
Activities of the Scottish Institute.	III	1972	290.2

INDEX TO TITLES

All references are made to part, date and item number. The titles, unless quotations, are arranged by first word not an article, and then by each subsequent word in alphabetical order.
a indicates that the work is an article, section (ii) of Parts II and III.
b indicates that the work is a biography, section (iii) of Part III.
sub indicates that the title is the sub-title of the work.

"A Careful and Most Ingenious Fabrication of Imaginary Accounts": Scottish railway accounts before 1868. W. Vamplew.	IIIa	1974	309.4
ABERDEEN shore works accounts, 1596-1670.	II	1596	219
ACCOMPT of expenses in Edinburgh by Alexander Rose ... 1715.	II	1715	241
ACCOMPT, the toun of Glasgow with Francis Stevenson, wright.	II	1703	236
ACCOMPTANT'S guide, The. J. Morrison.	I	1801	50
ACCOMPTANT'S pocket companion, The: a manual ... J. Drummond.	I	1718	11
ACCOUNT book of Sir John Foulis of Ravelston, 1671-1707.	II	1671	232
ACCOUNT for building a new road on Tyrebagger Hill ...	II	1759	247
ACCOUNT-keeping in principle and practice. G. Lisle and W.A. Middleton.	I	1911	173
ACCOUNT of pamphlets since June 1, 1704.	II	1704	239
ACCOUNT of the collector of tiends, 1703-1707. (Glasgow).	II	1703	237
ACCOUNT of the losses of the burgh of Dunbar, 1651. F.F. Roberts.	IIa	1651	260
ACCOUNT of the present state of the Hebrides and Western coasts of Scotland ..., An. J. Anderson. see	II	1785	249
ACCOUNT of the rotula arithmetica, An. G. Fisher.	I	1700	4
ACCOUNTANT 'CA' case, The ... J. Martin.	I	1896	139
ACCOUNTANT profession, The: a public danger ... J. Martin.	I	1895	136
ACCOUNTANT squabble, The: ... J. Martin.	I	1908	169
ACCOUNTANTS' clubs. A.B.G. Dunlop.	IIIa	1967	306
ACCOUNTANT'S digest, The ... J.B. Wardhaugh.	I	1904	158
ACCOUNTANT'S handbook of interest states ..., The. R.C. Millar.	I	1889	118
ACCOUNTANT'S magazine, The. Blackwoods publishing co.	I	1897	140
ACCOUNTANTS of excise. J.F. Mitchell.	IIIa	1965	303
ACCOUNTING in England and Scotland, 1543-1800. B.S. Yamey et al.	III	1963	285
ACCOUNTING in theory and practice ... G. Lisle.	I	1899	147
ACCOUNTS of Dr. Alexander Skene, The, ... D.H. Fleming.	IIa	1683	263
ACCOUNTS of St. Salvator's College ..., The. D.H. Fleming.	IIa	1679	262
ACCOUNTS of Sir Duncan Forestar of Skipinch, comptroller ...	II	1495	202
ACCOUNTS of Sir William Trussell.	II	1346	197
ACCOUNTS of the Chamberlains of Scotland ...	II	1329	196
ACCOUNTS of the collectors of thirds of benefices ...	II	1561	214
ACCOUNTS of the Great Chamberlains of Scotland ..., The.	II	1326	195
ACCOUNTS of the King's pursemaster, 1539-40.	II	1539	208
ACCOUNTS of the Lord High Treasurer of Scotland. (1473-1574)	II	1473	200
ACCOUNTS of the masters of works for ... royal palaces ...	II	1529	205
ACCOUNTS of the Treasurer of Scotland ..., The. (Continuation of Accounts of the Lord High Treasurer)	II	1473	200
ACCOUNTS of the treasurers of the royal burgh of Dumfries ... R.C. Reid.	IIa	1633	258
ACCURATE accomptants best companion, The. (sub) G. Fisher.	I	1717	10
ADVICE to tradesmen to learn bookkeeping, An. W. Stevenson. see	I	1756	24
ACTIVITIES of the Scottish Institute. S.A. Zeff.	III	1972	290.2
AESCULAPIUS in Fife: a study of the early 18th century. B. Seton.	IIa	1710	265

ALLEN'S forty lessons in practical double entry bookkeeping ... G. Allen.	I	1885	110
ANALECTA Scotica ... J. Maidment (editor) see	II	1659	229
see also	II	1704	239
ANTECEDENTS of Kidston, Jackson and co., The.	III	1969	289
ARITHMETIC, both in theory and practice ... J. Hill.	I	1764	32
ARITHMETIC, both in theory and practice. J. Hill.	I	app	186.1
ARITHMETIC in all its parts, vulgar and decimal ... W. Craighead.	I	1757	26
ARITHMETIC in the most plainest and most concise methods ... G. Fisher.	I	1756	23
ARITHMETIC modernised. J. Davidson and R. Scott.	I	1827	76
ARITHMETIC, rational and practical ... J. Mair.	I	1766	34
ARITHMETICA infinita. G. Brown.	I	1717	10
ARITHMETICK compendiz'd. D. Spence.	I	1714	8
ARITHMETICK in all its parts. (sub) J. Paterson.	I	1685	2
ART and practice of account keeping, The. J.C. MacCall.	I	1884	109
ARTHUR Young and the business he founded.	IIIb	1948	322
AYR burgh accounts, 1428-1429. G.S. Pryde.	IIa	1428	252
AYR burgh accounts, 1534-1624. G.S. Pryde.	II	1534	206
BALANCING for expert bookkeepers. G.P. Norton.	I	1894	131
BANK bookkeeping. D. M'Kie.	I	1900	150
BANKING and commercial arithmetic. D. M'Kie.	I	1912	177
BOOK containing tables for ... exchange ... and annualrents ..., A. A. Heriot.	I	1697	3
BOOK of annualrentaris and wedsettaris within the schirrefdome of Abirdein, The.	II	1633	225
BOOK of the farm, The. Henry Stephens.	I	1844	89.1
BOOK of the landed estate, The. Robert E. Brown.	I	1869	105.2
BOOKKEEPING and accountancy: Scottish practice ... D. Murray.	IIIa	1905	293
BOOKKEEPING as a specific subject ... J.D. MacLean.	I	1892	124
BOOKKEEPING by double entry ... (and) single entry. W. Lorrain.	I	1807	56
BOOKKEEPING by double entry exemplified ... J. Nelson.	I	1871	107
BOOKKEEPING by double entry explained. J. Findlater.	I	1900	149
BOOKKEEPING (by double entry) made easy ... J. Somerville.	I	1899	148
BOOKKEEPING by double entry reduced ... to one simple rule. W. Stevenson.	I	1762	29
BOOKKEEPING by single and double entry ... W. Inglis.	I	1849	91
BOOKKEEPING down to date. A. Munro.	I	1905	163
BOOKKEEPING for every business: ... A. Montgomerie.	I	1858	96
BOOKKEEPING for farmers.	I	1916	180
BOOKKEEPING for the classroom and counting house ... J.D. MacLean.	I	1857	95
BOOKKEEPING methodiz'd. J. Mair.	I	1736	19
BOOKKEEPING moderniz'd. J. Mair.	I	1773	37
BOOKKEEPING new modelled. W. Hamilton.	I	1735	18
BOOKKEEPING: observations and suggestions. A.M. Stuart.	I	1894	133
BREWERY accounts. K. Cook.	I	1906	164
BROWN'S ships' accounts and captain's letter writer ... J.W. Anderson.	I	1907	166
BUILDING society finance and statistics ... T.J. Millar.	I	1905	162
BUSINESS fact classified v. double entry ... T.J. Millar.	I	1916	181
BUSINESS of an accountant, The. J.A. Robertson.	I	1895	137
BUTTERWORTH'S young arithmeticians instructor ...	I	1805	53

CALCULATION and accountantship ... (sub) J. Scruton.	I	1777	41
CHAMBERLAIN's account, 1650, Dunnottar.	II	1650	227
CHAMBERS' bookkeeping ... W. & R. Chambers (publishers)	I	1892	123
CHAMBERS'S examination bookkeeping ... J. Bell.	I	1889	117
CHAPTERS in the history of bookkeeping, accountancy and commercial arithmetic. D. Murray.	III	1930	280
CHARTER of incorporation, bye-laws, rules and regulations. Chartered Accountants of Scotland.	I	1904	155.1
CHARTER of incorporation, rules, regulations and bye-laws. Chartered Accountants of Scotland.	I	1904	155.2
CHARTERED Accountants' Hall, Edinburgh. A.B.G. Dunlop.	IIIa	1966	304
CHARTERED Accountants of Scotland, The, 1854-1954. R. Browning.	IIIa	1954	296
CHECK figure systems ... A.H. Muir.	I	1909	170
CHECK numbers and other aids to balancing books ... T.J. Millar.	I	1907	167
CLEAR and distinct method by which persons ... may ... see what they have received ..., A. (sub) R. Hamilton.	I	1727	16
COCKER'S arithmetic ... revised by J. Mair.	I	1751	23
COCKER'S arithmetick, ... revised by G. Fisher.	I	1749	22
COMMERCIAL guide, The: systematic bookkeeping ... C. Lassen.	I	1891	120
COMPANY ACCOUNTING. Formation to balance sheet. J.D.C. MacKay.	I	1911	174
COMPENDIOUS but a compleat system of decimal arithmetic ..., A. G. Brown.	I	1701	6
COMPENDIUM of practical arithmetic ..., A. J. Morrison.	I	1814	64
COMPENDIUM of practical bookkeeping ..., A. J. Howatt.	I	1842	88
COMPLETE course of bookkeeping ..., A. C. Hutton.	I	1838	83
COMPLETE English Tradesman, The. Daniel Defoe.	I	1839	85.1
COMPLETE ready reckoner ..., The. J. Halliday.	I	1826	74
COMPLETE system of arithmetic ..., A. (sub) J. Davidson and R. Scott.	I	1827	76
COMPLETE system of merchant's accounts ..., A. J. Morrison.	I	1808	58
COMPLETE system of practical bookkeeping ..., A. C. Morrison.	I	1814	63
COMPLETE treatise on bookkeeping, A. C. Hutton.	I	1838	84
COMPLETE treatise on practical arithmetic and bookkeeping ..., A. C. Hutton.	I	1804	52
COMPLETE treatise on practical bookkeeping ..., A. J. Morrison.	I	1803	51
COMPTE buik of David Wedderburne ..., The.	II	1587	217
COMPTE of James Murray of Kilbertoun, Maister of Wark, ...The.	II	1628	224
COMPTROLLER, the, 1425-1488. A.L. Murray.	IIIa	1973	309
CONCISE system of practical arithmetic ... A. Melrose.	I	1791	47
CORPORATION finance. J. Colquhoun.	I	1894	128
COUNTING house manual, The. D. Taylor.	I	1838	85
COUNTING house manual and introduction to business ... 'Calculator'	I	1843	89
CUSTOMS accounts of Dumfries and Kirkcudbright ..., The. A.L. Murray.	IIa	1560	256
CUSTOMS accounts of Kirkcudbright, Wigtown and Dumfries, The. A.L. Murray.	IIa	1434	252.1
DAME Erskine's account book, 1678.	11a	1678	261
DAVID Murray, accounting historian ... E. Stevelinck.	IIIb	1928	321
DAY books of a Dumfriesshire draper ..., The. W.A.J. Prevost.	IIa	1810	274
DEED of constitution and rules or regulations. Institute of Accountants of Glasgow.	I	1853	91.1
DEPOSIT receipt interest tables. G. Lisle.	I	1888	116

DEVELOPMENT of accountancy in relation to commerce, The. T.P. Laird.	IIIa	1919	294
DIARY and general expenditure book of William Cunningham ..., The.	II	1673	232
DID the devil win the toss? J. Martin.	I	1897	142
DISSERTATION concerning the arithmetick of annuities, A. J. Innes.	I	1741	20
DRUMLANRIG estate-book, A, 1740-1745. R.C. Reid.	IIa	1740	272
DUMBARTON common good accounts, 1614-1660.	II	1614	223
DUMFRIES rental, A. G.W. Shirley.	IIa	1548	255
DUNCAN Dewar. A student of St. Andrews ... His accounts.	II	1820	250
EAST Lothian executor's account, An. A. Montgomerie.	IIa	1645	259
EASY bookkeeping for small co-operative societies ... G. Hines et al.	I	1897	115
EASY introduction to bookkeeping ..., An. J. Jamieson.	I	1835	82
EDINBURGH account book 200 years ago, An. J.G.A. Baird.	IIa	1699	264
EDINBURGH records. The burgh accounts.	II	1544	210
EDINBURGH treasurer's accounts, 1734-35.	IIa	1734	271
EDUCATION in Edinburgh in the 18th century. A. Law.	III	1965	286
EIGHTEENTH century audit, An.	IIIa	1923	295
EIGHTEENTH century Hawick farmer's rent ... book, An. R.E. Scott.	IIa	1730	269
ELEMENTARY bookkeeping. G. Lisle.	I	1894	129
ELEMENTARY bookkeeping for day and evening schools .. A.Munro.	I	1911	175
ELEMENTARY principles and rules of bookkeeping .. J.Morrison.	I	1810	59
ELEMENTARY treatise on bookkeeping by double entry ... D. Tolmie.	I	1885	112
ELEMENTS, analysis ... of arithmetic ... in ... business, The. W. Gordon and R. Dobson.	I	1771	36
ELEMENTS of bookkeeping in a series of short examples ... Ireland: Commissioners of National Education.	I	1863	101
ELEMENTS of bookkeeping in a series of short examples.	I	1864	102.1
ELEMENTS of practical arithmetic simplified, The. C.Morrison.	I	app	187
EMERGENT Professionals, The. Jas. C. Stewart.	IIIa	1975	309.6
EMINENT accountants of the past. see	IIIb	(310-319)	
ENCYCLOPAEDIA of accounting. G. Lisle (editor)	I	1903	152
ENGRAVED system of bookkeeping, An. C. Buchanan.	I	1808	57
ESSAYS on bookkeeping ... W. Webster.	I	1758	27
ESTIMATE for making a canal.	II	1785	249
EXAMINATION papers of the Chartered Accountants of Scotland. G. Lisle.	I	1894	130
EXAMINATION questions in bookkeeping by double entry ... J. Bell.	I	1867	105
EXCERPTS from the burgh accounts (Irvine).	II	1600	220
EXCERPTS from the household book of my Lord Archbishop of St. Andrews ...	II	1663	230
EXCHEQUER and Council in the reign of James V. A.L. Murray.	IIIa	1960	300.1
EXCHEQUER rolls of Scotland, The.	II	1264	193
EXHIBITION accounts and finance ... John M. MacLeod.	I	1903	154.1
EXPLANATION of Greig's accounting accuracy table .. W.M. Greig	I	1913	179
EXTRACTS from the account book ... 1659 ... Treasurer of ... Linlithgow ...	II	1659	229
EXTRACTS from the accounts of the burgh of Aberdeen (1398-1648)	II	1398	198
EXTRACTS from the accounts of the burgh of Edinburgh, 1552-1556.	II	1552	211
EXTRACTS from the accounts of the burgh of Glasgow, 1573-1714.	II	1573	215
EXTRACTS from the accounts of the burgh of Peebles, 1554-1661.	II	1554	212
EXTRACTS from the accounts of the burgh of Stirling, 1634-1752.	II	1634	226
EXTRACTS from the accounts of the common good ...	II	1557	213

FAILURE of the City of Glasgow Bank and the rise of independent auditing, The. R.E. Tyson.	IIIa	1974	309.3
FAIRBAIRN'S interest tables ... for ... current accounts. J. Fairbairn.	I	1861	100
FARM bookkeeping. W. Inglis.	I	1866	103
FARM bookkeeping and accounts. W.M. Price.	I	1916	182
FARMER'S account-book of expenditure ..., The. D. Young.	I	1790	46
FIRST Scottish book on accounting. R.H. Parker.	IIIa	1974	309.1
FIXED machinery. David Strathie.	I	1892	125.1
FLUCTUATIONS in security values ... W.S. Nicol.	I	1907	168
FORMS and powers of the Court of the Exchequer in Scotland ..., The. Sir J. Clerk and J. Scrope.	III	1820	276
FUNDAMENTAL principles and reasons for accompting by debitor and creditor. (2nd.ed. title) R. Lundin.	I	1718	12
GENERAL accountant, The. C. Morrison	I	app	188
GENERAL counting-house and man of business ..., The. W. Gordon.	I	1766	33
GENERAL discourse shewing the usefulness of the Italian method of bookkeeping ..., A. W. Stevenson.	I	1732	17
GLASGOW staff of the Royal Bank a century and a half ago, The	IIIa	1959	300
GLIMPSES of early accountancy in Glasgow. Sir J. Mann.	IIIa	1954	297
GOVERNMENT examination papers for leaving certificates ... J. Todd.	I	1894	134
GRAPHIC bookkeeping exercises. R. Scott.	I	1903	155
GREIG'S accounting accuracy table ... W.M. Greig.	I	1912	176
GUIDE to business and science for the use of schools ... (sub) R. Murray.	I	1830	78
GUIDE to farm-bookkeeping ..., A. I. Munro.	I	1821	70
HADDINGTON surgeon's account, 1611, A.	IIa	1611	257
HALYBURTON'S ledger and his times. F.A. Ritson.	IIa	1492	253
HANDBOOK to parish council finance, accounting ..., A. J.T. Maxwell.	I	1905	161
HARRIS estate papers, 1724-1754. A. Morrison.	IIa	1724	267
HISTORICAL accounting.	IIIa	1970	308
HISTORY of accounting and accountants, A. R. Brown.	(I	1905	159
	(III	1905	279
HISTORY of Cooper Brothers and co., 1854-1954.	III	1954	282
HISTORY of mathematical teaching in Scotland ..., The. D.K. Wilson.	III	1935	281
HISTORY of the Chartered Accountants of Scotland from earliest times to 1954.	III	1954	283
HOUSEHOLD account of Ludovick, Duke of Lennox ...	II	1607	221
HOUSEHOLD book of Lady Grisell Baillie, 1692-1733.	II	1692	225
HOUSE-keeping accounts, 17th century.	IIa	1674	261
HOWARD'S Anglo-American art of reckoning.	I	1888	115.1
IDEA rationaria. R. Colinson.	I	1683	1
IMPROVED system of arithmetic ..., An. (sub) W. Halbert.	I	1789	44
IMPROVED system of practical book keeping according to single entry ..., An. J. MacLaren.	I	1853	92

INCOME tax tables. G. Lisle.	I	app	192
INCOME tax tables. D. M'Kie.	I	app	190
INSTRUCTIONS for the collectors ... in Her Majesties' Customs ... accompting. Great Britain: Customs.	I	1707	7
INSTRUCTOR, The. G. Fisher.	I	1762	30
INTEREST at 4%. J. Marshall.	I	1823	72
INTEREST tables at 4%. J. Boaz and W. Jaffray.	I	1823	71
INTEREST tables ... for ... current accounts, Fairbairn's.	I	1861	100
INTEREST tables ... 1 to 10%, MacGregor's.	I	app	189
INTERIM account of a going concern ... Mann, Judd, Gordon and co.	III	1967	288
INTERVAL tables, interest tables, ... J. Boaz	I	1820	67
INTRODUCTION to arithmetick ..., An. J. Wilson.	I	1741	21
INTRODUCTION to bookkeeping and business ..., Charles Morrison.	I	1819	66.1
INTRODUCTION to counting house and examination bookkeeping ..., An. J.D. MacLean.	I	1892	125
INTRODUCTION to merchandise ..., An. R. Hamilton.	I	1777	40
INVENTORIES and account rolls (Priory of Coldingham)	II	1311	194
JAMES Beattie's day book, 1773-1798.	II	1773	248
JOHN Mair. M.J. Mepham and W. Stone.	IIIa	-	309.7
KING'S College dinner account of 1670, A.	II	1670	231
LAW relating to audits and auditors, The. J.M. Ross.	I	1894	132
LAWYER'S cash bookkeeping ... J.W. M'Clymont.	I	1890	119
LEDGER of Andrew Halyburton ..., 1492-1503, The.	II	1492	201
LIE triumphant in the law courts ..., The. (sub) J. Martin.	I	1897	142
LIFE and labour on an Aberdeenshire estate, 1735-1750.	II	1735	242
LIFE in a country manse about 1720. H.G. Graham.	IIa	1711	266
LOCAL Government (Scotland) Act, ... on the bookkeeping and forms of accounts ... G. Lisle.	I	1891	121
LOCHARKAIG treasure, The.	II	1746	245
LORDSHIP of Paisley, The, being the accompt ... 1757-1760.	II	1757	246
M'DOUGALL'S bookkeeping for elementary schools ... J.D.S. Bogal and J.H. Attfield.	I	1895	135
McDOUGALL'S exercises in bookkeeping. J. Barnetson.	I	1899	146
MacGREGOR'S interest tables ... W. MacGregor.	I	app	189
MacNEILL of Carskey, his estate journal, 1703-1743.	II	1703	238
MAN of business and gentleman's assistant, The. W. Perry.	I	1774	38
MANAGEMENT bookkeeping ... T.J. Millar.	I	1910	171
MANUAL of bookkeeping by double entry, A. W. Hardie and A. Allan.	I	1893	127
MANUAL of bookkeeping for law agents ... W. Hardie.	I	1893	126
MANUAL of commerce.	I	app	188.1
MANUAL of commerce ..., A. W. Waterston.	I	1840	86
MARINE engineering estimates and costs ... C.R. Bruce.	I	1911	172
MAUCHLINE account books of Melrose Abbey, 1527-1528. Margaret H.B. Sanderson.	II	1527	204.1
MEDIEVAL Scots merchant's handbook, A. A. Hanham.	IIa	1400	251
MERCHANT-accounts by double entry ... (sub) J. Mair.	I	1773	37
MERCHANT'S companion, The, ... being a way for making up accompts ... W. Newall.	I	1715	9
MERCHANT'S, tradesman's and family's assistant, The. (sub) J. Thomson.	I	1784	42

METHOD of farm bookkeeping ..., A. A. Trotter.	I	1825	73
METHODICAL treatise of merchant-accompts ..., A. (sub) J. Mair.	I	1736	19
MONTHLY interest tables at 1, $1\frac{1}{2}$ and 2%. D. M'Kie.	I	1885	111
MR. Treasurer, Edinburgh - before 1835. H. Armet.	IIIa	1956	298
NEAL'S synopsis of bookkeeping ... Neal.	I	1912	178
NEW century bookkeeping for business people. R. Scott.	I	1901	151
NEW system of commercial arithmetic, A. R. Murray.	I	1830	78
NEW system of practical arithmetic for ... men of business, A. W. Scott.	I	1782	41.1
NEW treatise of arithmetic and bookkeeping ..., A. A. Malcolm.	I	1718	14
NOTE on the principles of bookkeeping ... T.J. Millar.	I	1906	165
OCHERTYRE house book of accompts, 1737-1739.	II	1737	244
ODD time tables. W.A. Robertson and A. Fisher.	I	1919	184
OFFICIAL directory. Scottish Chartered Accountants.	III	1896	278
OLD day-book, An. J. Byers.	IIa	1814	275
ON a new ... plan. Tables for calculating interest ... John Smith.	I	1810	60
ON life assurance bookkeeping ... J.J. MacLauchlan.	I	1891	122
OPENING address (to) the Aberdeen ... Students ... J. Meston.	I	1886	113
ORGANISATION of gold-mining business ..., The. N. Brown.	I	1897	141
ORIGIN and present organisation of the profession of	(I	1869	106
chartered accountancy in Scotland, The. J. McClelland.	(III	1869	277
ORIGINS of the break-even chart: Sir John Mann, The. R.H. Parker.	III	1969	290
PANARITHMOLOGIA. W. Leybourn.	I	1761	28
PERFECT accomptant, The. (sub) R. Colinson.	I	1683	1
PHILOSOPHY of arithmetic ..., The. <u>Sir</u> J. Leslie.	I	1817	66
PLEASING art of money-catching.	I	1840	85.2
POCKET guide to commercial bookkeeping, The. R. Wallace.	I	1847	90
PORTIONS of rentals ... household books and inventories of Breadlebane.	II	1582	216
POWIS papers, 1507-1894.	II	1736	243
PRACTICAL book-keeping ... C. Buchanan.	I	1806	54
PRACTICAL bookkeeping adapted to commercial and judicial accounting ... F.H. Carter.	I	1861	99
PRACTICAL counting house, The. J. Scruton.	I	1777	41
PRACTICAL figurer, The. W. Halbert.	I	1789	44
PRACTICAL introduction to life and fire assurance ..., A. T.H. Millar.	I	1841	87
PRACTICAL system of farmers bookkeeping ..., A. (sub) A. Farquharson.	I	1813	61
PRACTICAL treatise on arithmetic arranged for pupils ..., A. R. Stewart.	I	1853	94
PRESIDENTIAL address (on history) Campbell.	IIIa	1897	292
PRE-UNION records of the Scottish Exchequer, The. A.L. Murray.	III	1973	290.3
PRINCIPLES and practice of double entry bookkeeping ..., The. (sub) D. Taylor.	I	1838	85
PRINCIPLES of arithmetic explained ..., The. A. Ingram.	I	1826	75
PRINCIPLES of bookkeeping explain'd ..., The. A. MacGhie.	I	1718	13
PRINCIPLES of double entry bookkeeping explained ..., The. R. Little.	I	1903	153
PRINCIPLES of life annuities and assurances ... An Accountant.	I	1829	77
PROCEDURE of the Scottish Exchequer ..., The. A.L. Murray.	IIIa	1961	301
PROFESSION in Scotland, The: a retrospect. J. Howden.	IIIa	1894	291

QUALIFICATION for membership a hundred years ago.
Jas. C. Stewart. IIIa 1974 309.2

RAILWAY accounts and their audit. A.F. Dodd. I 1904 156
READIEST reckoner in miniature ..., The. J. Thomson. I 1815 65
REASON for accompting by debitor and creditor ..., The.
R. Lundin. I 1718 12
RECONSTRUCTION of Braemar and Cogarff castles ..., The.
J.M. Bulloch. IIa 1748 273
RECORDS of a Scottish cloth manufactory at New Mills ...,
The. II 1681 234
RENTAL accounts made easy. R. Hamilton. I 1727 16
RENTAL book of the Cistercian abbey at Coupar-Angus ... II 1443 199
RENTAL book of the diocese of Glasgow, 1509-1570. II 1509 204
RENTAL of feuduties and annualrents payable to the burgh
of Glasgow. II 1657 228
RENTAL of the prebendary of the altar of St. Mary ... II 1543 209
RENTALE Dunkeldense, being the accounts of the bishopric ... II 1505 203
RENTALE Sancti Andree, being the chamberlain ... accounts. II 1538 207
RENTALL of the burgh and city, 1590. (Glasgow) II 1590 218
RENTALS of Strathavon. II 1608 222
REPORT of the trial ... against the Directors and Manager
of The City of Glasgow Bank. C.T. Couper. III 1879 277.1
REVENUE of the Scottish Crown, 1681. Sir William Purves. II 1681 234.1
REVENUES of the Bishopric of Moray ..., The. A.L. Murray. IIa 1538 254
RICHARD Brown, President of the Society of Accountants in
Edinburgh. IIIb 1918 320
ROXBURGHSHIRE mansion and its contents in 1729, A.
A.O. Curle. IIa 1729 268
ROYAL charter ... and bye-laws, rules and regulations.
Chartered Accountants of Scotland. I c.1867 105.1
RULES and forms ... regulating the keeping of accounts ...
Edinburgh: General Board of Lunacy. I 1883 108
RURAL accountant, The. A. Farquharson. I 1811 61

SANCTIFICATION of the lie, The, ... J. Martin. I 1897 143
SCANDAL at the Edinburgh Stamp Office, The. B.E.V. Sabine. IIIa 1975 309.5
SCOTS arithmetician, The. J. Paterson. I 1685 2
SCOTTISH Accountant, The. I 1895 137.1
SCOTTISH chartered accountants. A.B.G. Dunlop. IIIa 1965 303.1
SCOTTISH Treasury, 1667-1708, The. A.L. Murray. IIIa 1965 303.1
SCOTT'S new bookkeeping guide. R. Scott. I 1919 185
SELECTIONS from the Monymusk papers, 1713-1755. II 1713 240
SERIES of improved mercantile forms and accounts ..., A.
C. Morrison. I 1860 98
SERIOUS advice to tradesmen ... the inconveniencies ... by
not learning bookkeeping, A. W. Stevenson. I 1756 25
SET of books adapted to MacLaren's book keeping ...
J. MacLaren. I 1853 93
SHORT set of bookkeeping by double entry ..., A. D. Brodie. I 1831 79
SHORT system of arithmetic and bookkeeping ... R. Hamilton. I 1796 48
SHORT treatise on arithmetick ..., A. (sub) D. Spence. I 1714 8
SIMPLE system of bookkeeping for farmers ..., A.
D.G. MacDonald and J. Grant. I 1918 183

SIMPLE interest tables. D. M'Kie.	I	app	191
SINCE 1954.	IIIa	1968	307
SINGLE entry bookkeeping. W. Inglis.	I	1866	104
SIR JOHN SKENE and the Exchequer, 1594-1612. A.L. Murray.	III	1971	290.1
SOME notes on the early literature and development of cost accounting in Great Britain - III. R.S. Edwards.	IIIa	1937	295.1
SOME suggestions in regard to life office accounting ... A.D.L. Turnbull.	I	1898	145
SOME topics in the history of financial accounting in England, 1500-1900. B.S. Yamey.	III	1962	284
SPECIE book ... to turne any ... piece of silver ... to pounds ..., A. G. Brown.	I	1700	5
SPECIMENS of working records and account books ... N. Brown.	I	1896	138
STEPS in the evolution of the profession in the U.K.	IIIa	1957	299
TABLES for calculating interest at 5%. John Smith.	I	1810	60
TABLES of annualrent or simple interest ... James Smith.	I	1718	15
TABLES of compound interest and annuities ... A.H. Turnbull.	I	1863	102
TABLES of compound interest and annuities ... D. M'Kie.	I	1903	154
TABLES of interest at 3, 4, 4½ and 5% ... J. Morison.	I	1789	45
TABLES of interest at 3, 4, 4½ and 5%. J. Thomson.	I	1768	35
TABLES of interest for the use of bankers and others. T. Smith.	I	1785	43
TABLES of simple and compound interest ... John Laurie.	I	1776	39
TABLES of simple interest and commission ... W. Stenhouse.	I	1806	55
TABLES of simple interest computed decimally ... T. Dunn.	I	1821	69
THREE topics in the history of accounting. R.H. Parker.	IIIa	1966	305
TRADERS sure guide, containing tables ..., The. (sub) W. Leybourn.	I	1761	28
TRANSACTIONS see under the name of the society in the author index.			
TREATISE of merchants' accounts ..., A. (sub) W. Hamilton.	I	1735	18
TREATISE on arithmetic, in theory and practice ..., A. R.C. Stewart.	I	1834	81
TREATISE on bookkeeping by double and single entry, A. J. Bryce	I	1860	97
TRIAL of the City of Glasgow Bank Directors. W. Wallace (editor).	III	1905	279.1
TWO eighteenth century tailors. S. Maxwell.	II	1732	270
'UNISPECT' system of bookkeeping, The. A.T. Hunter.	I	1905	160
UNIVERSAL accountant and complete merchant, The. W. Gordon.	I	1763	31
UNIVERSAL calculator, The. J. Thomson.	I	1784	42
WILSON, Stirling and co., 1864-1964.	III	1964	287
WRITINGMASTER and accountant's assistant ..., The. C. Buchanan.	I	1798	49
YOUNG arithmetician's guide ..., The. J. Davidson.	I	1834	80
YOUNG estate manager's guide, The. R. Henderson.	I	1898	144
YOUNG ladies' guide to practical arithmetic and bookkeeping ..., The. J. Morrison.	I	1813	62
YOUNG lady's guide to practical arithmetic ... keeping accounts, The. C. Morrison.	I	1820	68
YOUNG man's best companion, The. (sub) G. Fisher.	I	1763	30
1912 et seq. - a personal interim report. A.G. McBain.	IIIb	-	323
218 St. Vincent Street, Glasgow. A.G. McBain.	IIIa	1964	302

Printed and Published in Great Britain by The Accountants' Publishing Co. Ltd.
for The Institute of Chartered Accountants of Scotland

ADDENDA

PART I

DILWORTH, Thomas. 1782

The Schoolmaster's assistant, being a compendium of arithmetic both practical and theoretical. Paisley: 1782.

REF: -
LOC: -

-----(another edition). Glasgow: 1798.
LOC: Library of Congress.

-----(another edition). Ayr: J. & P. Wilson, 1800.
LOC: NLS; AUL; EUL; Newcastle Univ.; Leeds School of Education Museum.

-----(another edition). Ayr: 1804.
LOC: Harvard.

-----a new edition. Edinburgh: 1816.
LOC: GUL.

This book was originally published in London. T. Dilworth (died 1780) was also the author of the immensely popular "The Young Book-keeper's Assistant: shewing him ... the Italian way of Stating Debtor and Creditor", first published in mid-18th century, reaching its 26th edition before the end of the century and still being published in the 1870s (still calling double entry the Italian method).

INSTITUTE OF ACCOUNTANTS AND ACTUARIES IN GLASGOW. 1889

Catalogue of the books in the library of the Institute of Accountants and Actuaries in Glasgow. Glasgow: 1889.
(Not seen)

-----2nd.ed. William Hodge & Co., for the Institute, 1906.
334p. 25cm.
REF: -
LOC: SE.

This dictionary catalogue (subject and author) covered articles as well as books and general subjects as well as accounting.

MURRAY, David. 1909

Solicitors' accounts and accounting, with a bibliography. Glasgow: Incorporated Society of Law Agents, 1909.
20p. 8vo.
REF: -
LOC: NLS; Library of Congress.
See also items 280, 293, 321 and below.

SOCIETY OF ACCOUNTANTS IN ABERDEEN. 1927

Catalogue of books in the library. Aberdeen: Society of Accountants in Aberdeen, 1927.
46p. 22cm.
REF: -
LOC: SE.

SOCIETY OF ACCOUNTANTS IN EDINBURGH. 1902

Catalogue of the books in the Library of the Society at 27 Queen Street, Edinburgh. Edinburgh: T. & A. Constable, for the Society, 1902.

88p. 22.5cm.

REF: -

LOC: SE.

PART III

(iii) Biographies.

MURRAY, Sylvia W. 1933

David Murray: a bibliographical memoir. Dumbarton: Bennett & Thomson, 1933.

52p. 23cm.

REF: -

LOC: NLS; BM.

------(another edition). 1936.

LOC: NLS.

By the daughter of the author of items 293 and 280 (and see item 321).

For Product Safety Concerns and Information please contact our
EU representative GPSR@taylorandfrancis.com Taylor & Francis
Verlag GmbH, Kaufingerstraße 24, 80331 München, Germany